Teeth 'n' Smiles

Teeth 'n' Smiles

A play by
DAVID HARE

FABER AND FABER
London · Boston

First published in 1976
by Faber and Faber Limited
3 Queen Square London WC1
Reprinted 1979
Printed in Great Britain by
Latimer Trend & Company Ltd Plymouth
All rights reserved

ISBN 0 571 10995 0

All rights whatsoever in this play are strictly reserved and applications for permission to perform it, etc. must be made in advance, before rehearsals begin, to Margaret Ramsay Ltd., 14a Goodwin's Court, St Martin's Lane, London WC2. The music of the songs by Nick Bicât and the lyrics by Tony Bicât are reproduced by kind permission of Riderwood Ltd., c/o First Composers Co., Pinewood Studios, Iver Heath, Buckinghamshire, to whom application must be made for permission to perform them.

for Joe

Of Mr Blake's company I have very little. He is always in Paradise.

Mrs William Blake

Characters

ARTHUR	songwriter
INCH	roadie
LAURA	p.r.
NASH	drummer
WILSON	keyboard
SNEAD	porter
PEYOTE	bass guitar
SMEGS	lead guitar
ANSON	student
MAGGIE	vocals
SARAFFIAN	manager
RANDOLPH	star

Teeth 'n' Smiles, with music by Nick Bicât and lyrics by Tony Bicât, was first performed on 2 September 1975 at the Royal Court Theatre, London. The cast was as follows:

ARTHUR	Jack Shepherd
INCH	Karl Howman
LAURA	Cherie Lunghi
NASH	Rene Augustus
WILSON	Mick Ford
SNEAD	Roger Hume
PEYOTE	Hugh Fraser
SMEGS	Andrew Dickson
ANSON	Antony Sher
MAGGIE	Helen Mirren
SARAFFIAN	Dave King
RANDOLPH	Heinz

Directed by the author
Designed by Jocelyn Herbert

The play is set during the night of 9 June 1969.

The playing area is mostly bare. Design is minimal. The band's equipment is on a stage which, for the musical numbers, trucks down to the front. In the first act the band are housed in a college room; in the second they are on a lawn behind their stage.

NOTE

When *Teeth 'n' Smiles* was first played it ran just under three hours. It was then cut during previews to what the English think is a more palatable length. This text accommodates most of those cuts, but not all of them. The text was further re-written for a West End production. I don't think plays are ever finished, and the version you read is one of several.

The chorus from the song 'How Do You Do It?' by Mitch Murray is reprinted by kind permission of Dick James Music Ltd. © 1962. The lines from Cole Porter's 'You're the Top' from the musical production *Anything Goes* are used by permission of Harms Inc. Chappell & Co. © 1934. For the quotation from W. B. Yeats on page 57 acknowledgements are due to Mrs W. B. Yeats and MacMillan & Co. Ltd. Details of the bombing of the Café de Paris can be found in *The Blitz* by Constantine Fitzgibbon (Corgi).

SCENE ONE

As the audience come in INCH *is building the amplifiers into a bank of equipment on the band's platform. He is twenty, in leather and jewellery. Downstage there are a couple of benches, representing an undergraduate's room that has been specially emptied.* ARTHUR *is lying on one bench, staring. He is wearing a silver top hat and a silk suit but the effect is oddly discreet. He is tall, thin and twenty-six.*

    INCH *disappears.*

    The play begins.

    INCH *comes in carrying two suitcases which he puts down in the middle of the room.*

INCH: Right. Let's smash the place up.

    (*He turns and sees* ARTHUR.)

    'Allo, Arfer, din know you was comin'.

ARTHUR: Motorbike. How is she?

INCH: All right. They're liftin' 'er out the van now.

    (INCH *goes out.*)

ARTHUR: You're the top, you're the Coliseum

        You're the top, you're the Louvre Museum

        You're a melody from a symphony by Strauss . . .

    (INCH *returns with a Samuelsons box from which he takes a plug. Then* LAURA *appears, a small dark girl with lovely skin.*)

LAURA: Are you set up, Inch, it's very late?

INCH: Got Maggie out?

LAURA: They're getting her down the drive.

ARTHUR: And hello, Laura.

LAURA: And hello, Arthur. Some bastard put sugar in the petrol tank, that's why we're late.

ARTHUR: It's good to see you.

LAURA: How long can you stay?

ARTHUR: How long do you want?

LAURA: Well . . .

(WILSON, *a small, bearded cockney, and* NASH, *a spaced-out black drummer, appear, look round the room and sit down.* WILSON *gets out a bottle of green lemonade.* LAURA *begins to unpack the bags she has brought in.*)

ARTHUR: Saraffian said he thought she might be on the way down.

LAURA: How Saraffian's meant to know, sitting in that office all day . . .

ARTHUR: He has a manager's nose. He's like a truffle pig, he can smell heroin at fifty paces.

LAURA: Don't be absurd, dumbo. It's not smack, it's booze. Liquid boredom. Twice a day she flips out.

WILSON: Game.

NASH: Wot's it to be?

WILSON: Pope's balls. The game is the most borin' and useless piece of information you can think of. Thus the Pope 'as balls.

NASH: Right.

WILSON: Away you go.

(LAURA *arranges a series of dresses on the back of the bench. Then starts sewing one of her choice.*)

NASH: The town of Nottingham was once called Snottingham.

WILSON: Yeah, that's borin'.

NASH: Thank you, pal, your go.

(INCH *returns with eight bottles of scotch, which he sets out on a bench.*)

WILSON: Efrem Zimbalist's first wife's name was Alma Gluck.

NASH: Well done, Wilson, that's really dull.

INCH: Diana Dors' real name was Diana Fluck.

NASH: Hello, Arthur.

ARTHUR: Nashy. How are you?

INCH: Or Diana Clunt, I can't remember which.

WILSON: The capital of Burundi is Bujumbura.

INCH: Or possibly Diana Clocksucker, but I think I would've remembered that.

(INCH *goes.*)

LAURA: She starts drinking at breakfast, she passes out after lunch, then she's up for supper, ready for the show. Then after the

show she starts drinking. At two-thirty she's out again.
Morning she gets up. And drinks. She's a great professional.
Never misses a show.

ARTHUR: Pills?

LAURA: No.

ARTHUR: Reds?

LAURA: No. Blue heavens, no. Yellow jackets, no. Bennies, no. No
goofballs, no dexies, no dollies.

ARTHUR: Still no acid?

LAURA: No.

ARTHUR: And the heroin?

LAURA: No. She just drinks.

ARTHUR: What is she, some kind of pervert?

(PEYOTE *enters with an electric kettle and sits down. A moment
later* INCH *appears with an extension cable from the stage, and
they plug the kettle in.*)

LAURA: No aeroplane glue, no household cement, no banana peel,
no fingernail polish remover, no nutmeg, no paintstripper. No
one in the world but her and Johnny Walker.

ARTHUR: And the singing?

LAURA: The singing's O.K.

(LAURA *goes out.* INCH *hails* SNEAD *who is carrying* MAGGIE
into the room over his shoulder. SNEAD *is forty-five, in
top hat and black tails, this side of his first coronary. We do
not see her.*)

INCH: Waiter, can you take 'er up to a bathroom?

SNEAD: Sir.

ARTHUR: You're the Nile
You're the Tower of Pisa
You're the smile
On the Mona Lisa . . .

(SNEAD *has taken* MAGGIE *away.* PEYOTE *arranges a plastic
funnel and two glass tubes, which he then sets out with care on
the bench.* NASH *gets up.*)

NASH: And where the 'ell are we?

(*Pause. Then he starts changing his shirt.* INCH *begins mending a
plug.*)

WILSON: At this moment in time on planet earth the dead outnumber the living by thirty to one.

(LAURA *returns, distributing pork pies.*)

LAURA: She doesn't speak very warmly of you.

ARTHUR: I'm not meant to drag round the country, am I?

LAURA (*smiles*): Or of me.

ARTHUR: Still sings my songs.

LAURA: She'd prefer not to.

ARTHUR: I'm sure.

LAURA: She'd prefer to get up there and scream.

ARTHUR: You're a Moscow view
　　　　You're oh so cool
　　　　You're Lester Young . . .

(SMEGS *appears. He is dressed like a very baggy matelot. He never raises his voice.*)

SMEGS: Couple of slags here say anyone fancy a blow-job?

(ARTHUR *gets up as if to consider.*)

ARTHUR: A blow-job. Do I want a blow-job?

LAURA: How did they get in here?

SMEGS: Inch? Blow-job?

ARTHUR: Bound to turn out like a Chinese meal. Half an hour later and you need another.

INCH: Butterfly flicks, do they do butterfly flicks?

SMEGS: Ask them.

INCH: Sure.

LAURA (*to* PEYOTE): Do you have to do that in here?

PEYOTE: Fuck off.

INCH (*laughs*): But will they do butterfly flicks with a roadie?

(*He goes to find out.*)

SMEGS: Not a chance.

ARTHUR: Isn't he meant to be . . .

SMEGS: What?

ARTHUR: Setting up. You're an hour late.

LAURA (*holding a dress up*): Does this look all right?

SMEGS: It's up to him.

ARTHUR: Why don't you go and help him?

SMEGS: Because we're artists.

ARTHUR: All right.

SMEGS: See?

14

LAURA: Artists don't set up.

SMEGS: You don't ask Oistrakh to go out and strangle the cat.

(INCH *reappears, picks up the plug.*)

INCH: They do blow-jobs wiv singers, but nothin' below bass guitar.

ARTHUR: That's right, love, keep your standards up.

PEYOTE: I play fuckin' bass guitar.

(*He hurries out.*)

SMEGS: Artists. I mean. Keith Moon's chauffeur got run over, he said chauffeurs are two a penny, it's blokes like me what are irreplaceable.

WILSON: There is no word in the English language as rhymes with 'orange'.

NASH: Hey, these valiums, do they go with my shirt?

(*He tosses one in.* SNEAD *reappears.*)

SNEAD: Is that to be everything, sir?

INCH: No, you gotta get 'er clothes off and get 'er into the bath.

SNEAD: Sir?

INCH: You think I'm jokin'?

(*He heads out, his arm round* SNEAD.)

INCH: I'm doin' you a favour. You should be a member of the stevedores' union.

SNEAD: Sir?

INCH: We're gonna 'ave to wash 'er. Do you wanna know wot that's like?

SNEAD: Sir?

INCH: Well, 'ave you ever seen 'em cleanin' St Paul's?

(*They go out.*)

ARTHUR: Is that what happens every day?

(LAURA *just looks at him.*)

ARTHUR: What does everyone do?

LAURA: Pretend not to notice, what would you do?

ARTHUR: What . . .

LAURA: There's no choice. Stoke tomorrow. Then Keele. Bradford. Southampton. Quick one in Amsterdam. Back to Glasgow. Then they claim California, but nobody believes it.

ARTHUR: Saraffian's mad.

LAURA: Not Saraffian's idea. It's her. She wants to hit San

Francisco on her knees.

ARTHUR: What's the money?

LAURA: A hundred and twenty, no more. It won't cover overheads, whatever it is. But she . . . likes to keep busy.

SMEGS: All this jumping on the spot makes you feel famous. But it's no real substitute for people knowing your name.

(SMEGS *goes out.*)

WILSON: Arfer.

ARTHUR: Yes.

WILSON: Your contribution.

(*Pause.*)

ARTHUR: H. G. Wells was attractive to women because his breath smelt of honey.

(*Pause.*)

WILSON: Very nice.

NASH: I enjoyed that.

WILSON: Very nice.

(ANSON *appears. He is nineteen, unusually short with long frizzy black hair. He carries a clipboard and wears evening dress with a velvet bow tie.*)

ANSON: Are we nearly . . .

ARTHUR: There's a plug.

ANSON: What?

ARTHUR: We're waiting to mend a plug. Look. Over there.

(*They look at the plug.*)

ARTHUR: And then we'll be ready.

ANSON: I'm the organizer. The booking. You are . . . ninety minutes late you know. Couldn't someone . . . one of you mend it yourselves?

ARTHUR: Arms like penguins I'm afraid.

ANSON: I see.

(*He goes out.* PEYOTE *reappears with a piece of gauze.* INCH *and* SNEAD *appear.*)

NASH: Three-quarters of all children are born before breakfast.

INCH: 'Ave you got 'er dress?

LAURA: Here. Tonight Miss Frisby is in peach.

SNEAD: Will that be everything, sir?

INCH: Why not lie down there and I'll walk all over yer?

16

SNEAD: Sir.

INCH: Jus' can't get any decent room service round 'ere.

(*He goes out.* LAURA *cuts a pork pie neatly in four.*)

NASH: Every time we breathe we inhale several million molecules that was exhaled by Leonardo da Vinci . . .

WILSON: No, no, Nashy.

NASH: Wot?

WILSON: You don' understand, that's really quite interestin', Leonardo, I mean, it's far too interestin' . . .

ARTHUR: I'm thinking of marketing a pork pie, a new kind of pork pie, which when you put the knife through the pastry will let out an agonized honk, as of a pig being slaughtered. It would do well.

(*He looks at the hovering* SNEAD.)

ARTHUR: A tip is it Mr Snead, is that what you're after?

SNEAD: Sir?

ARTHUR: Don't look at us, pal, we're too famous, we're like the Queen, we don't carry actual money.

SNEAD: Sir?

WILSON: An' you're playin' it far too fast.

(INCH *calls from offstage.*)

INCH: She says will Arfer 'elp 'er out the bath?

PEYOTE: Waiter.

SNEAD: Sir?

PEYOTE: Fuck off.

(ARTHUR *pulls at an imaginary dog on a lead.*)

ARTHUR: Come on, Arthur, come on boy, come and meet Maggie. Come on, come on boy.

(ARTHUR *and* SNEAD *go out different ways.* PEYOTE *sterilizes the tubes with boiling water which he then throws on the floor.*)

PEYOTE: Wot's that creep doin' 'ere?

LAURA: If . . .

PEYOTE: Never said it.

(*Pause.*)

LAURA: Where the others?

PEYOTE: I 'ate Canterbury. Every time we come to Canterbury I swear never to come again.

LAURA: So do I. Except this is Cambridge.

PEYOTE: Yeah. Look.

(PEYOTE *holds up a fresh hypodermic in a sterilized packet*.)

PEYOTE: The cleanest needle in showbiz.

LAURA: T'rific.

WILSON: It should be *dull*.

PEYOTE: The bag.

LAURA: What?

PEYOTE: The bag. Pass me the bag.

LAURA: This is Maggie's.

PEYOTE: Pass me the fuckin' bag.

(LAURA *hands the carpetbag to* PEYOTE. *He lightly tears the lining. Takes out an envelope*.)

PEYOTE: Jus' borrowed 'er bag.

LAURA: That . . .

PEYOTE: Uh. Jus' borrowed 'er bag.

(ANSON *returns*.)

ANSON: Has there been any . . .

LAURA: Progress? No.

PEYOTE: She en't bin busted as often as me.

LAURA: That would be quite hard, Peyote. I mean, you would have to stand on street corners stuffing tabs up traffic wardens' nostrils to get yourself busted quite as often as you.

PEYOTE: Fuck off.

ANSON: Is Miss Frisby with you?

LAURA: She's just being sandblasted next door. Why don't you sit down?

ANSON: Thank you.

(ARTHUR *wanders back*.)

LAURA: Did you see her?

ARTHUR: What is she on?

LAURA: Huh, did she recognize you?

ARTHUR: She said, who let this pieca shit in here?

LAURA: She recognized you.

ARTHUR: Yes.

LAURA: I must call Saraffian. Do you know where there's a phone?

ANSON: In the porter's . . .

LAURA: Lodge? Thank you.

ARTHUR: He doesn't care. As long as they stagger on to the stage.

18

Get their hands somewhere near the guitar. Yes, Peyote?

PEYOTE: Fuck off.

ARTHUR: I don't care either. Butcher my tunes. Forget my lyrics. Steal my royalties. I expect it.

(*Pause.*)

Thought she . . . thought she wanted to see me.

LAURA: Sure.

ARTHUR: Just tell me what she's on.

LAURA: Arthur, you lived with her . . .

ARTHUR: Have you let her get hooked? Well? Have you let her get hooked again?

LAURA: Have I?

ARTHUR: Well?

(LAURA *storms out, furious.* ARTHUR *turns away.* PEYOTE *has melted twenty pills in boiling water and is now pouring them through the funnel and gauze into the other tube.* WILSON *and* NASH *are flat out, probably asleep, possibly concentrating.*)

ANSON: Have you had a look where you're . . .

(*Pause.*)

ARTHUR: Peyote, do you know what she's on?

PEYOTE: She's mainlinin' string. Pullin' it through 'er veins.

ANSON: Do you want to have a look at . . .

ARTHUR: Little fella, why don't you ever get through a . . .

ANSON: Sentence. I know. It's . . . I just hear what I'm saying and it always sounds so dreary and second-hand I just am . . . too fastidious to . . .

ARTHUR: Finish.

ANSON: Right.

(*Pause.*)

I'm hoping to interview Miss Frisby.

ARTHUR: She's in the bathroom, walk right up.

ANSON: Does she have any clothes on?

ARTHUR: It's never stopped her before.

ANSON: Ah.

ARTHUR: What you going to ask her?

ANSON: Oh . . . general things. About the role of popular music in society.

(*Pause.*)

ARTHUR: Yes, well, that's a very good subject. Very good subject. You could even ask Peyote here about that. He has a lot of words to say on that. Well, not a lot. Acually he has two. Off and fuck. Only usually he contrives to put them the other way round.

(ARTHUR *goes out.* PEYOTE *and* ANSON *are now as if alone.* PEYOTE *ties a rubber tube round his upper arm, teases the liquid in the hypodermic.* ANSON *is embarrassed.*)

ANSON: Hmph.

PEYOTE: Ah.

(ANSON *gets up and moves away.* PEYOTE *shoots up.*)

ANSON: Squeamish. Grotesquely squeamish for a medical student. It's a problem. Really. You call that shooting up?

PEYOTE: Uh-huh.

ANSON: Is that heroin?

PEYOTE: Preludin.

ANSON: Ah. Preludin is a fuck-pump, I think I'm right. I know that much. It enlarges your sexual capacity. You're meant to stay hard for twenty-four hours, is that not . . . I believe that's right.

(*Pause.*)

It's none of my business but I think you may be taking rather a chance. I mean in Cambridge. Knowing the overall standard of skirt in this town I'd say twenty minutes would be pushing your luck.

(*Pause.*)

I had a guitar once. When I was young. Had a guitar. And a drum.

(*Pause.*)

You make conversation seem a little unreal. I suppose the silence is what . . . turns you on.

(*Pause.*)

Yes. I know. Fuck off. Certainly. By all means.

(*He moves towards the plug.*)

PEYOTE: Don't touch it.

(INCH *returns.*)

INCH: Right.

ANSON: Are you nearly . . .

NICH: Jus' gotta change this plug.

ANSON: Will it take very long?

INCH: Don't know, it's a technical thing.

ANSON: Is it going to be good tonight?

(*Pause.*)

INCH: It's gettin' really nasty out there.

ANSON: What?

INCH: The audience. They're stamping all over the lawn.
Fuck.

ANSON: What?

INCH: Forgotten the flowers.

(INCH *goes out again, putting the plug down.* SNEAD *appears at the same time.*)

ANSON: Are you . . .

SNEAD: Everyone's now ready for the orchestra, sir.

INCH: Tell 'em they're jus' gettin' inta their dickies.

(INCH *gone.*)

SNEAD: I think you'll have to make some announcement, sir.
They're getting very restless having to wait.

ANSON: Tell them . . . er . . . tell them they're coming just as fast
as they can.

(ARTHUR *comes on, goosing* LAURA *who is wearing his top hat
and laughing.*)

ANSON: Ah . . . do you think they're almost . . .

ARTHUR: Listen, they got the place right, didn't they? That's
three-quarters of the battle. The time, the time is a
sophisticated detail.

ANSON: I don't know, Mr Snead.

PEYOTE: Wot is this place, anyway?

ARTHUR: You are in what scientists now know to be a black hole,
Peyote. Floating free, an airless, lightless, dayless, nightless
time-lock, a cosmic accident called Jesus College Ball.

PEYOTE: Jesus.

ARTHUR: College Ball.

PEYOTE: What does it mean?

ARTHUR: It means the college at which I was educated. Yes, Mr
Snead?

LAURA: It means undergraduates.

ARTHUR: Narcissists.

LAURA: Yahoos.

ARTHUR: Intellectuals.

(ARTHUR *embraces* LAURA *from behind, his hands on her breasts.*)
Rich complacent self-loving self-regarding self-righteous
phoney half-baked politically immature neurotic evil-
minded little shits.

(*He stares at* SNEAD.)
Expect nothing and you will not be disappointed.

(*Silence.* SNEAD *turns and goes out.* ANSON *looks at his hands.*
ARTHUR *turns his back to us.*)

WILSON: Internal memorandum. Rhyl Town Hall. The life
expectancy of a civic deck chair is now a season and a half.

LAURA: He used to clip tickets.

ARTHUR: I was at this college. I know Mr Snead of old. Give me
that.

(LAURA *gives him her current cigarette.*)
Where I first met Maggie. She was singing in the Red Lion.
She was sixteen, seventeen, a folk singer. Let us go a pickin'
nuts, fol de ray, to Glastonbury fair, a tiddle dum ay. I had to
carry her over the wall, can you imagine, to get her to my
rooms. They build walls here to stop undergraduates making
love. Well, we got caught, of course, by this very Mr Snead
coming in satirical German manner, even shining a torch, an
English suburban stormfuhrer. He hauled me up to my
tutor, who said, do you intend to marry the girl? I said, not
entirely. He said, as this is a first offence you will not be sent
down, instead I fine you ten pounds for having a girl on the
premises. I said what you mean like a brothel charge? I was
furious, I was out of my mind. Do you have another?

(LAURA *lights him another.*)
Thanks. And everyone told me: don't waste your energy.
Because that's what they want. They invent a few rules that
don't mean anything so that you can ruin your health trying
to change them. Then overnight they re-draft them because
they didn't really matter in the first place. One day it's a
revolution to say fuck on the bus. Next day it's the only way
to get a ticket. That's how the system works. An obstacle

course. Unimportant. Well, perhaps.

(*Pause. He stands a moment.*)

NASH: The word Cicero literally means chick-pea.

ANSON: Oh God. I think I'd better . . . go and . . .

LAURA: Don't. Don't go away.

ARTHUR: Sit down, tell us something about yourself.

ANSON: I'm sorry. It's just so late. I . . .

ARTHUR: People appreciate things more when they've had to wait.

ANSON: That's not how we advertised . . .

ARTHUR: Let them suffer.

ANSON: We didn't sell the tickets on the quality of the suffering
we could offer.

ARTHUR: Well done. Whole sentence. This band has converted
more people to classical music than any other human form of
torture.

ANSON: I don't understand why . . .

ARTHUR: They come out saying, please, please, give me a drip in a
bucket.

(INCH *returns.*)

INCH: She says she's not going on tonight.

ANSON: Oh no.

ARTHUR: Uh, it's fine. Don't panic.

INCH: It's quite all right, it's fine.

ARTHUR: The nights she's not going on are fine. It's the nights she
can't wait to get on, they're the ones to watch for.

WILSON: Right.

(INCH *goes.* SMEGS *wanders back on.*)

SMEGS: How we doing?

LAURA: Fine.

ARTHUR: Fine.

WILSON: Fine.

SMEGS (*sits*): Must be almost time.

ANSON: Yes.

WILSON: Only one man 'as actually died on television. In a
television studio. 'E was on a stool, talkin' about 'ealth food,
about honey, an' 'e jus' fell over an' died.

NASH: Fantastic.

WILSON: Yeah.

23

(PEYOTE *stretches out.*)

PEYOTE: It's so good, it's so very good . . .

SMEGS: I wouldn't have minded a sound check.

ARTHUR: When did you last have one of those?

SMEGS: Barnsley. Halifax. I don't know. They carry me about in a
sealed container. And sometimes the seasons change. Or we
run over a dog. Or they change the design on my cigarette
pack.

ARTHUR: Well . . .

SMEGS: I don't know.

ARTHUR: It seems to be what she wants.

SMEGS: It's needless you know. It just makes her feel good.

ARTHUR: How is she to you?

LAURA: Unspeakable.

ARTHUR: Ah.

LAURA: She treats me barely human.

ARTHUR: Still?

LAURA: More than ever. She is jealous.

ARTHUR: I don't see . . .

(PEYOTE *sits up suddenly. Panic.*)

PEYOTE: There's a wheel comin' off the van.

ARTHUR: It's all right, Peyote, it's just a brain cell dying.

PEYOTE: It's comin' off.

SMEGS: It'll be horses in a minute, on sweeties he always has
horses.

ANSON: I'm sorry but I really do have to insist . . .

WILSON: What is wrong with you?

ANSON: I . . .

WILSON: I don't think I've ever met a man wiv so little karma.

ANSON: How can I . . .

WILSON: You should leave your brain to a Buddhist 'ospital, they'd
be very interested in you.

ANSON: We are waiting for one plug to be connected.

WILSON: Correct.

ANSON: It's ridiculous.

WILSON: Don't touch it.

ANSON: It's absurd.

(*Pause.*)

ANSON: I'm sorry, I just can't . . .
(ANSON *moves towards the plug*.)
WILSON: Don't fuckin' touch it, you miserable little turd.
(*Pause*.)
ARTHUR: Just leave it to Inch.
LAURA: Inch changes a mean plug.
WILSON: Right.
ARTHUR: Inch is a great roadie. Inch is the Panama Red of roadies.
ANSON: I'm . . .
ARTHUR: Just . . .
(*He holds up his hands. Pause*.)
It's just best. O.K.?
(INCH *returns*.)
INCH: She says she's goin' on.
ARTHUR: Ah.
INCH: She says she can't wait to get out there.
ARTHUR: Fine.
INCH: Now. What? I'm almost ready. There was somethin'.
ANSON: Plug.
INCH: I jus' gotta change this plug.
ARTHUR: Fine. No hurry. Enjoy it.
(INCH *sets to. Then stops*.)
INCH: I can't work if I'm watched.
(ANSON *turns away*.)
WILSON: A pullet is a pullet till the first time it moults. Then it's a
hen.
SMEGS: Sussex have never won the County championship.
NASH: Marilyn Monroe was colour blind.
ARTHUR: Oscar Wilde died Sebastian Melmoth.
WILSON: Two gallons to one peck. Four pecks to one bushel.
Eight bushels to one quarter. Four and a half quarters to a
chaldron. One hectolitre per hectare equals one point one
bushels per acre.
INCH: Right. Ready when you are.
ANSON: I think we're ready.
INCH: O.K., band?
WILSON: You might plug it in first, then we'll join yer.
INCH: Fine.

25

(INCH *goes*.)

WILSON: Not gonna walk across there if the plug's not gonna work.

NASH: Get yer sneakers dirty.

WILSON: Quite.

ANSON: Well, everyone . . . let me say . . . go out there and break
a leg.

(ANSON *goes*.)

WILSON: Wot an 'orrible little man.

NASH: 'E's very *short*, in' 'e?

WILSON: Yeah, an' that 'orrible black 'air. Makes 'im look like a
lavatory brush.

SMEGS: Are we playing outside?

LAURA: Yes. On the lawn.

WILSON: Wot if it rains?

ARTHUR: Somebody had better . . .

SMEGS: Yes.

ARTHUR: Peyote.

(ARTHUR *wakes him*.)

PEYOTE: Horses.

SMEGS: Told you.

WILSON: Come on, Peyote, once through the Christmas oratorio.

NASH: You take one arm.

WILSON: Yeah, come in loud, eh Nashy? Drum all over 'im if you
find 'e's on the floor.

NASH: Will do.

PEYOTE: Horses poundin' down the Mall.

WILSON: Right, right, Peyote.

SMEGS: Off we go.

(PEYOTE *is guided towards the stage. The rest drift with him.
They disappear behind the equipment*.)

WILSON (*as he goes*): I wish we'd found somethin' more, well,
more kinda staggeringly borin'.

(ARTHUR *and* LAURA *left on their own*.)

LAURA: Are you going to watch?

ARTHUR: What?

LAURA: Arthur.

ARTHUR: Yes, of course.

LAURA: I'll see you later.

ARTHUR: Good.

LAURA: Arthur. Don't drift away from me.

(*She goes.* ARTHUR *alone at the front. Then at the back you see* INCH *raise his arm. He is holding the mended plug.*)

ARTHUR: Paganini played the violin so well . . . people said he was in league with the devil.

(*The plug goes in. The music crashes on.*)

The First Set

The band's truck rolls downstage, the music already on the way. The band is PEYOTE (*bass*), WILSON (*keyboard*), SMEGS (*lead*), NASH (*drums*). *Standing about watching and talking are* INCH, LAURA *and* ARTHUR. *The band sing by themselves.*

Close To Me

In a cafe called Disaster
Photos of the movie stars
Looked down upon the customers
As if they came from Mars
In a cafe called Disaster
Shelter from the rain
You said you couldn't love me
That we should never meet again

Will you always be this close to me
When you're far
When you're far
When you're far away from me
And will you always
Will you always be this close to me
When you're far
When you're far
When you're far away from me
And will it always be the same

In an age of miracles
In the heat of the afternoon
Falling on your funny face

27

The shadow of the moon
In an age of miracles
As sharp as any knife
I felt a touch of winter
In the summer of my life

And will you always etc.

(*Then without a break the band go straight into the next number.
Dazzling light.* MAGGIE *joins them, singing, burning off the fat as
she goes.*)

CLOSE TO ME

In a ca-fe called Dis-as-ter Photos of the mo-vie stars. Looked
down up-on the cus-tom-ers As if they came from Mars
In a ca-fe called Dis-as-ter Shel-ter from the rain
You said you couldn't love me That we should ne-ver meet a-gain.
Will you always be this
close to me When you're far When you're far When you're far a-
-way from me And will you al-ways Will you al-ways be this
close to me When you're far When you're far When you're far a-
-way from me And will it al-ways be the same.

28

Passing Through

Mamma said I had the morals
Of an alley cat
Just because I wanted more
Sister fuckin' Rita
Was a mean child beater
But she said I was a high street whore

Burning down the freeway
Like a shootin' star
Bitching how my life is run
Learning how to shake it
In the back of a Bedford
Taking it from every mother-fucker's son

Shut your mouth honey
I don't wanna know your name
Shut your mouth honey
I don't care why you came
Pass me the bottle
Roll over let's do it again

Say you gotta save it
For someone special
And you know that that's a lie
If you don't holler
When the lights go out
Life is gonna pass you by
Gotta reputation as a
One night stand
Kinda precious too
If you let a greaser
Stay another night
They're gonna get a lease on you

Shut your mouth etc.

I'm a sunflower lady
With a sweet electric band
I'm a sunflower lady
With a bottle and a man
Don't want quiet
I don't want care
When the sun comes up
And the lights blaze out
If you don't scream honey
How do they know you're there

(*The truck goes back almost before the song ends.* ARTHUR
wanders down and sits quietly at the front.)

PASSING THROUGH

SCENE TWO

ARTHUR *sits staring out front. Then* WILSON *and* NASH *come in, both fuming to a standstill.*

ARTHUR: Sorry about that.

WILSON: Necrophilia. Like fuckin' the dead.

NASH: Amateur night at 'Arrods staff canteen.

WILSON: Like floggin' a corpse.

NASH: The bastards.

WILSON: Fuck 'em.

NASH: Bastards.

(SMEGS *comes in.*)

SMEGS: What bastards.

WILSON: Do you know, some woofter comes up to me after the set, says I expectin' somethin' altogether more Dionysiac, I says Thursdays we're Dionysiac, Fridays we're jus' fuckin' awful.

ARTHUR: Right.

WILSON: Not that I care.

NASH: Right.

WILSON: Fuckin' penguins.

ARTHUR: Right.

WILSON: I'm sittin' there, I'm thinkin' the Marshall Stack's up the spout an' the Vox AC30 'as gone on the blink, an' not even the cloth-ears of Cambridge are fooled.

ARTHUR: And that's just the first set.

NASH: Right.

WILSON: 'Ow long till the next one?

ARTHUR: One o'clock. And the last at three-thirty. Then you can go to bed.

(NASH *hands out joints.* INCH *comes in carrying a guitar which he sets about mending.*)

NASH: And you . . .

INCH: Sorry, lads, bit o' wobble on the Vox.

NASH: Wobble?

NCH: I've smeared it with pork fat, usually does the trick.

(ANSON *appears*.)

ANSON: I've come to interview Maggie. She told me . . .

WILSON: Last month in Miami, Florida . . .

NASH: Again.

ANSON: . . . to wait here.

WILSON: Jim Morrison of the Doors got it out. Not the only occasion this 'as 'appened. By no means. There is the example of our own P. J. Proby in the Croydon Odeon, splittin' 'is velvets from knee to crotch.

SMEGS: A great moment.

WILSON: The. Great. Moment.

ARTHUR: Yes.

WILSON: Slightly spoilt, it must be said, by the fact 'e then spontaneously split 'em every night till 'e was thrown off the tour.

ARTHUR: A mistake.

WILSON: Certainly. That bit. A mistake.

NASH: That's right.

(*Pause.* WILSON *inhales deeply*.)

WILSON: Fuck 'em. An' I know 'ow 'e feels.

ANSON: How do you think it went?

(*Silence. They all smoke.* MAGGIE *appears talking from a long way off.* LAURA *dancing attendance*.)

MAGGIE: Mother born in Hitchin, father born in Hatfield, so they met half way and lived all their life in Stevenage. That's how my interview begins.

ARTHUR: Oh, Jesus.

(NASH, WILSON, SMEGS *and* INCH *rise as a man, and leave as quickly as they can*.)

MAGGIE: Guess I must have been unhappy as a child . . .

ARTHUR: Oh, my God.

MAGGIE: Laura, I would love something to eat.

LAURA: Sure.

(LAURA *goes off*.)

MAGGIE: Well, hello, Candy Peel, I thought it was you.

ARTHUR: Hallo, Maggie.

MAGGIE: Do you know why I call him Candy Peel? Because he has

34

a small scrap of that substance hanging where real men . . .

ARTHUR: Thank you, Maggie, do the same for you.

MAGGIE: Do you know how you survive in Stevenage? You say this isn't happening to me. That's what you say. You say I may appear to be stifling to death in this crabby over-heated mausoleum with these cringing waxworks who claim to be my parents. But it's not true. I'm not here. I'm really some way away. And fifty foot up.

ARTHUR: Right.

MAGGIE: In fact I'm a Viking.

ARTHUR: Have you got this?

ANSON: I . . .

ARTHUR: I would write it down if I were you.

MAGGIE: In another age. I was a Viking. Reincarnation. I had a dream last night, I was called Thor, and I was wrapped in furs and I had strips of dried meat tied round my waist.

ARTHUR: Well, I think we can guess what the dried meat means, honey.

MAGGIE: No nourishment in Stevenage. You draw no strength. It's like living on the moon.

ANSON: I have heard you saying that before.

MAGGIE: Listen, kid, you ask for an interview, I give you an interview. If you wanna *new* interview you gotta pay more, understand?

ANSON: Yes. Sorry.

MAGGIE: Like to rub my back, Arthur?

ARTHUR: Give me the bottle.

MAGGIE: I won't drink before the show, Arthur. I just like to hold it, O.K.?

(*Pause.*)

MAGGIE: Ask us another question.

ANSON: Would you say . . .

MAGGIE: Yes?

ANSON: Would you say the ideas expressed in popular music . . . have had the desired effect of changing . . . society in any way?

(*Pause.*)

MAGGIE: Hamburger. Dill pickle. That's what I want.

(LAURA *returns with* SNEAD.)

LAURA: I got the gay boy back.

ARTHUR: Ah, come in, waiter.

MAGGIE: Hallo, ringer, must have been you in the tub just now.

SNEAD: Sir?

ARTHUR: Did you say sir?

MAGGIE: That's all right, I'm just one of the boys.

ARTHUR: Hamburger, please, Mr Snead. With dill pickle.

MAGGIE: And relish and french fries. Coca-cola. And a banana
pretty. And a vanilla ice with hot chocolate sauce. Chopped
nuts. And some tinned peaches. And tomato sauce for the
hamburger. With onion rings. And mayonnaise. And
frankfurters. Frankfurters for everyone, O.K.? With French
mustard. And some toasted cheese and tomato sandwiches.
With chutney. On brown bread, by the way, I'm a health
freak.

ARTHUR: Got that, Mr Snead?

SNEAD: I'm afraid I'll have to send out for this. Do you think you
could give me some money?

LAURA: Money?

MAGGIE: Don't make with the jokes, ringer, they don't go with the
grovelling.

SNEAD: I can get you something from the college kitchen.

ARTHUR: O.K., just get us whatever's nice and greasy and
answers to the name of Rover, O.K.?

SNEAD: Sir?

MAGGIE: Then the first time I heard Bessie Smith, that was
somethin'.

ARTHUR: Off you go.

SNEAD: Sir.

(SNEAD *goes out.*)

MAGGIE: That was really somethin'. In a record shop, I was
fourteen. Did you know that as well?

ANSON: Actually I . . . read your press release.

MAGGIE: Did you?

(*Pause.*)

LAURA: I reckoned he should . . .

MAGGIE: Yes, well I do have some sort of life outside my press

release. I can't remember where I put it, but I do know I
have it.

(MAGGIE *gets up and slips the scotch bottle back in the rank of
eight.*)

LAURA: Do you want to change for the next set?

MAGGIE: What you gawpin' at?

ANSON: Looking at you.

(MAGGIE *points to where she had been sitting.*)

MAGGIE: Still looking at the tragedy? That was over there. The
girl with no life of her own. I left her over there.

ANSON: That easy?

MAGGIE: Tragedy's easy. I pick it up, I sling it off. Like an over-
coat.

(*Pause.*)

ARTHUR: What is she on?

LAURA: Arthur.

ARTHUR: Will somebody please tell me what this girl is on?

(*Pause.*)

MAGGIE: So I tell you the story of my life. Everyone in Stevenage
hated me, they hated me when I was a child. Cos I was big
and fat and rich and took no shit from anyone. What's this
for?

ANSON: A university paper.

MAGGIE: So they sent me to a convent. Anything you heard about
randy nuns, forget it. They have tits like walnuts and
leathery little minds. But me, I'm like a great slurpy bag of
wet cement waiting to be knocked into shape. Everybody at
the convent, they hate me too.

ANSON: You . . .

MAGGIE: How did I lose it, is that what you want to know?

ANSON: I didn't . . . get . . .

MAGGIE: I lost it to an American airman on top of a tombstone in
Worthing cemetery. He was very scared. I was only thirteen
and he didn't want to lose his pilot's licence. Write this down
for Chrissake, it's good.

(ANSON'*s pencil obeys.*)

MAGGIE: So then even the American gets to hate me, yes, Laura?

LAURA: Oh, yes.

37

MAGGIE: She was at school with me, you see. We both had it, this English education. Takes a long time to wipe that particular dogshit off your shoe.

ANSON: And Arthur?

MAGGIE: Arthur I meet when I'm seventeen. A case of Trilby. Which is Trilby? I never know.

ARTHUR: The woman is Trilby.

MAGGIE: And the monster is Frankenstein.

ARTHUR: No.

MAGGIE: The doctor is Frankenstein.

ANSON: The monster doesn't have a name.

LAURA: The man is Svengali.

MAGGIE: Anyway. He invents me.

(ARTHUR *smiles and shrugs*.)

LAURA: Do you want to change?

MAGGIE: Yeah, I'll change.

(LAURA *organizes a new dress from the bags*.)

ANSON: Are there . . . any other singers you greatly admire?

MAGGIE: Well, it's a funny thing you'll find . . . singers mostly admire Billie Holliday, same as jazzmen admire Charlie Parker. Conductors say they admire Toscanini. It's something to do with how they're all dead.

ARTHUR: No competition.

MAGGIE (*smiles*): Yes.

ANSON: Among the living?

(MAGGIE *stands behind* ANSON *and puts her hands on his shoulders*.)

MAGGIE: This is all real you know, kid. None of the others can say that. Never had a nose-job. Or a face-lift. Or my chin pushed in. Or my jaw straightened. No paraffin wax, no mud-packs. All my own teeth. This is it. The real thing. I am the only girl singer in England not to have been spun out of soya bean.

ANSON: You never seem very happy to have been English. What would you rather have been?

MAGGIE: American.

ANSON: Why?

(MAGGIE *smilesat* ARTHUR.)

MAGGIE: America is a crippled giant, England is a sick gnome.

38

(ARTHUR *makes an o with his fingers.*)

MAGGIE: I sing of the pain. Do you understand?

ANSON: No.

MAGGIE: The words and music are Arthur's but the pain is mine. The pain is real. The quality of the singing depends on the quality of the pain.
(*Pause. She smiles.*)

MAGGIE: Yeah. What you study?

ANSON: Oh . . . medicine.

MAGGIE: Great.

ANSON: Well, yes, in a way except I don't seem very suited. It's not my . . . anyway . . . I don't want to bore you with my problems.

MAGGIE: What would you like to be?

ANSON: Well . . . I don't know. If I was free . . .
(MAGGIE *stares at him.*)

MAGGIE: Round the back of the Odeon? Yes? After the show? Would you like that?

ANSON: Odeon?

MAGGIE: It's a figure of speech. Kid.

ARTHUR: You could stand on a beerbox, reach up to her.

LAURA: Shake hands with Saigon Charlie.
(MAGGIE *smiles at them. Then cuffs lightly the top of* ANSON's *hair.*)

MAGGIE: First man I knew played rock music, he was nobody, a real nothing. I say rock music, but really it was all that hoopla and fag dancing the groups used to do. This boy got his big break, bottom of the bill with the Who, national tour. At the end of the tour he came back to Stevenage, he threw it in. I said, you got depressed because they're so good? He said, I got depressed because they're so very good, and yet even they ask the same questions I do every night: where is the money and where are the girls?
(*Pause.*)
And that is it. Where indeed is the money? And where are the girls?
(*Silence.* PEYOTE *walks into the room and lies down, says nothing.*)

MAGGIE: You know Jimi Hendrix gets depressed, he gets livid,
because he says people don't come to hear his music, not
really to listen, but simply because they've all heard he's got
a big cock and plays the guitar with his teeth.

ARTHUR: Yar.

MAGGIE: And I say, sure Jimi, you're right to complain, people are
cunts, but wouldn't it be a better idea to stop wearing tight
trousers and give up clapping your mouth round the strings?

LAURA: I think I'd better keep an eye on Peyote tonight.

MAGGIE: He'll be O.K.

LAURA: He may need looking after.

MAGGIE: If it makes you feel good.

(*Pause.*)

MAGGIE: The hat.

LAURA: What?

MAGGIE: I'd like that hat, Laura. Gonna wear that hat tonight.

(LAURA *hands it to her.*)

MAGGIE: Does Peyote have any chicks lined up?

ARTHUR: He didn't say so.

MAGGIE: Well, where's he gonna put it then?

ARTHUR: Can't guess.

MAGGIE: Can't go around with blue balls all night. Laura.

LAURA: I get sentimental about my body. Maggie. Everything else
I give to the band, but the body . . . you know . . . I still like
to choose.

(MAGGIE *laughs, turns to* ANSON.)

MAGGIE: You couldn't make her with a monkey wrench. Arthur
will tell you all about . . .

LAURA: End of interview.

MAGGIE: Laura here is my press secretary.

LAURA: End of interview. Anything else you need to know . . .

(MAGGIE *rides in over her, definitive.*)

MAGGIE: I only sleep with very stupid men. Write this down. The
reason I sleep with stupid men is: they never understand a
word I say. That makes me trust them.

(ARTHUR *gets up, moves away, turns his back.*)

So each one gets told a different secret, some terrible piece of
my life that only they will know. Some separate . . . awfulness.

But they don't know the rest, so they can't understand. Then the day I die, every man I've known will make for Wembley stadium. And each in turn will recount his special bit. And when they are joined, they will lighten up the sky.

(*She picks up the dress* LAURA *has laid out.*)

MAGGIE: Come on, kid, I'll change after. No point in getting another dress dirty.

ANSON: No.

(*She leads* ANSON *out. On the way they pass* SNEAD *wheeling in a huge trolley of steaming food. Salvers, tureens, etc.*)

LAURA: Hey, Maggie, the food.

MAGGIE: Not hungry.

(*She and* ANSON *go out.*)

LAURA: Just . . . leave it there will you, Mr Snead?

SNEAD: Madam.

LAURA: And thank you.

(SNEAD *goes.*)

ARTHUR: She knows exactly what she's doing. Always. That's what I learnt.

LAURA: Yes.

ARTHUR: She knows the effect she's having. Even when she's smashed, when she's flat out on the floor, there is still one circuit in her brain thinking, 'I am lying here, upsetting people.'

LAURA: Yes.

ARTHUR (*smiles*): There you are.

LAURA: Arthur.

(INCH *reappears with* NASH, *then* WILSON. *They check the place.*)

INCH: 'As she gone?

ARTHUR: Yes.

INCH: All right everyone, you can come out now.

LAURA: The little fellow with her.

ARTHUR: She swallowed him up like a vacuum cleaner.

(LAURA *dips a plastic cup in the tureen, drips green lumps of soup on the floor.*)

INCH: Did she tell the Jimi Hendrix gag?

LAURA: Of course.

INCH: Did she say . . .

41

LAURA: Yes, she said it.

INCH: You 'aven't 'eard it yet.

LAURA: I haven't heard it but she said it. Just terrible.

NASH: 'I sing of the pain.'

LAURA: She said that.

INCH: 'The pain is real.'

NASH: The pain is bloody real.

INCH: Mostly in the arse.

ARTHUR: All right.

(PEYOTE *gets up from the bench and leaps into the air. At the last moment he catches hold of an iron bar across the roof. He hangs there swinging slightly, eight feet above the ground, joint between his teeth.* WILSON *appears and opens a large book.*)

WILSON: Readings from the London telephone directory.

INCH: Oh no.

WILSON: The game is:

INCH: No.

WILSON: The game is: I read from the London telephone directory. You lot remain completely silent. The first person to make a sound is disqualified. The winner is the person who can stand it longest.

ARTHUR: Oh, my God.

WILSON: Arfer, you'll get yerself disqualified before we begin.

ARTHUR: Is that a . . .

WILSON: Now, where shall I begin? I think I was jus' gettin' inta the Smiths . . .

(SARAFFIAN *enters. He is in his early fifties with a paper hat, camel hair coat and streamers round his neck.*)

SARAFFIAN: Saraffian comes.

(*He releases a balloon full of water which squirts away into the air.*)

SARAFFIAN: And at once we have a party.

ARTHUR: Saraffian. My God.

(RANDOLPH *follows on. He is heavily made up, you cannot tell his age. He is carrying a crate of champagne.* SARAFFIAN *takes a chicken from inside his coat.*)

WILSON: 'Ello, Boss.

SARAFFIAN: Poulet farci aux champignons. Loot from the ball, my dears. And twelve bottles of a bleak little non-vintage Dom Perignon. Za za.

INCH: Fantastic.

NASH: Za za.

SARAFFIAN: Just in case we don't get paid. Wilson, you old dog, I've come to show you this . . . thing.

(*He gestures at* RANDOLPH.)

Put the crate down. Come here. Look. Look at my glittering pigeon-chested youth. How do you like it? My future star.

(*They all look at* RANDOLPH.)

NASH: Great.

SARAFFIAN: Beautiful, isn't it? I'm really proud. He's going to wipe up the queer market, no question.

RANDOLPH: I . . .

SARAFFIAN: Uh, don't risk it, just don't spoil it, lad. Don't mess with the words, O.K.? Don't risk them, they only get you into trouble.

RANDOLPH: Pl . . .

SARAFFIAN: He wants to protest his heterosexuality. Just don't mention it, underplay it and we might believe in it. Might.

(*Pause.*)

Much better. So. Hallo, Peyote, don't bother to come down, just stay up there if you want. So. I'm a fine surprise.

LAURA: Saraffian.

SARAFFIAN: My dear.

LAURA: What are you up to?

SARAFFIAN: Come to hear the band.

LAURA: I've been trying to ring you these last few days.

SARAFFIAN: Ah.

LAURA: Have you seen her?

PEYOTE: The sun goin' da'an. A tha'asand golden chariots. Leather. Metal. Horseflesh. Careerin' da'an through the sky.

(*He drops from the beam simply to the floor.*)

PEYOTE: Ten tha'asand angels in a single file.

LAURA: Have you seen her?

SARAFFIAN: Well . . .

WILSON: Did you 'ear the first set?

SARAFFIAN: Certainly I heard it. I heard it all. From beginning to

43

end. And I'm hoping it will have earned me some small remission in hell.

(*to* RANDOLPH.)

Look lively, open the bottles, son.

LAURA: When are you going to talk to her?

SARAFFIAN: Well, this is nice. Peyote, I saw your old woman last night. Would you believe it, she has another husband, she's still only nineteen.

WILSON: Wot's 'e like?

SARAFFIAN: Very charming. Easygoing bloke. Nose-flute player in a monastery band.

LAURA: She's not very well, Saraffian.

NASH: Let's 'avva game.

SARAFFIAN: Snap.

WILSON: Poker.

NASH: Monopoly.

WILSON: Lost the board.

LAURA: Saraffian.

WILSON: And Peyote swallowed the boot.

SARAFFIAN: Poker.

LAURA: And she's drinking again.

SARAFFIAN: Yes.

LAURA: Arthur will you tell him?

ARTHUR: I . . .

LAURA: Why do you think she drinks?

SARAFFIAN: I never ask, in my profession you expect to spend a portion of your time sitting by a hospital bed . . .

LAURA: Listen . . .

SARAFFIAN: I've got very good at it. I think the ultimate accolade of my profession should not be a disc, it should be a golden hypodermic.

LAURA: Saraffian.

SARAFFIAN: What is this? I pay a courtesy call on one of my bands . . .

LAURA: Don't be stupid. Courtesy call. When did you last see a band on the road?

SARAFFIAN: Glen Miller, I think.

LAURA: Saraffian, why does she drink?

44

SARAFFIAN: Why do we discuss her all the time? That's why she drinks. So we'll discuss her. You know, so we won't have time to do things like cut our fingernails or make love to our wives. That's why she drinks. So as to stop any nasty little outbreaks of happiness among her acquaintances. Are there any glasses for this stuff?

(INCH *goes to get some.*)

LAURA: So tell me why you thought Arthur should come.

SARAFFIAN: Kid.

ARTHUR: Please.

LAURA: Why does he have to come and see her again, it only screws her up.

SARAFFIAN: Please leave it, Laura, there are no answers and there is absolutely no point in the questions.

LAURA: I see. Can I say anything at all?

SARAFFIAN: No.

LAURA: Can anyone say anything?

SARAFFIAN: No.

(*A long pause.*)

I'm very grateful, Laura, for all the work you've done.

LAURA: Don't crawl up my arse, Saraffian, what is Arthur doing here?

SARAFFIAN: He . . .

ARTHUR: I wanted to come.

LAURA: What?

SARAFFIAN: He wanted to see her.

LAURA: Arthur?

SARAFFIAN: His own idea.

ARTHUR: Yes. Just to see her for Chrissake. I wanted to see her. Is that . . . just to see her.

(ARTHUR *goes out. A pause.*)

SARAFFIAN: Everyone should love everyone. Take the global view, Laura, please. Champagne.

(INCH *back with beer mugs.* SARAFFIAN *pours out.* LAURA *as if about to cry.*)

Ease up will you, Laura, you're doing Joan Crawford out of a job.

LAURA: Listen . .

45

SARAFFIAN: Shit, Laura, a man can love two women at once. I've seen it done. The human heart. Shall we ever understand it, Tone?

RANDOLPH: I . . .

SARAFFIAN: The answer is no. The boy adored her. Now he feels responsible. So.

(LAURA *gets up. Moves. Stops dead. The rest are sitting, staring into their mugs. Almost all comprehensively stoned now.*)

WILSON: And . . .

LAURA: Well . . .

INCH: There.

(*Pause.*)

SARAFFIAN: Look at it this way, Laura. I knew a Viennese teacher who said that desperate people who try to kill themselves but only succeed in shooting their eyes out, never, ever attempt suicide again. It's the sense of challenge you see. Once you've lost your eyes, it gives you something to live for.

(*He laughs.*)

PEYOTE: Dubbin. Brass. Bells.

NASH: Wot's up wi' 'im?

PEYOTE: Streakin' through the sky. The 'ouse'old cavalry itself.

WILSON: 'E's on 'orses again.

PEYOTE: Pomades. The royal 'orses.

WILSON: Said in the paper seventy per cent of adult males dream regularly of fuckin' Princess Anne.

INCH: Quite right. I mean, what's a royal family for if not to . . .

WILSON: . . . dream.

(*They smile. Pause.*)

PEYOTE: An' a cry of 'allelujah.

(SARAFFIAN *sits back. They all drowse.*)

LAURA: It's just possible anywhere, any time to decide to be a tragic figure. It's just an absolute determination to go down. The reasons are arbitrary, it may almost be pride, just not wanting to be like everyone else. I think you can die to avoid cliché. And you can let people die to avoid cliché.

SARAFFIAN: Quite.

(*Pause.*)

WILSON: Shall we play the telephone game?

SARAFFIAN: I can't tell you the beauty of this profession. Years ago when I was young. It was full of people called Nat and Harry and Dick in brown suits and two-tone shoes. With thick chunky jewellery as if someone had splattered hot melting gold over their bodies with a watering can, and it had set in great thick blobs. And golden discs on the walls. And heavy presentation ballpoint sets, on their desks. Would sell you their grandmother's wooden leg; Nat did sell his grand-mother's wooden leg, after she died, admittedly. And they muttered the totem phrases of the trade like, 'Tell him I'll get back to him.' There was no higher compliment an initiate could be paid than to be taken out for pickled brisket and beetroot borscht and be told in perfect confidence, 'The real dough's in sheet music. My son.' And they snapped great white fingers round the piano and used words like 'catchy' and 'wild'. And the artists . . . the artists bore no connection to the world I knew. When Nat travelled he carried them in the back of the van with a sliding glass compartment between him and them so he wouldn't have to listen to their conversation. He talked about installing sprinklers, as in Buchenwald. It was organized crime. Really. Those days. That's what interested me. The blatancy of it. The damnfool screaming stupidity of popular music. I loved it.

(*Pause. His eyes are closed.*)

You want me to sack her, you all want her to go.

(*Pause. He opens his eyes.*)

You are making the Mafia sign.

(*Pause. Nobody moves a muscle.* LAURA *looks furious.*)

O.K.

(*The band's equipment comes down silently and* SCENE TWO *scatters.*)

SCENE THREE

The abandoned stage. Just LAURA. *She walks behind the bank of speakers. She gets out a packet of fags. Lights two. Hands one down behind the amplifiers where it disappears. She moves away.*

LAURA: Where the people?

MAGGIE'S VOICE: In the dinner tent.

LAURA: Ah.

MAGGIE'S VOICE: They're having dinner. In the dinner tent.

(LAURA *goes behind the organ, picks up the clean dress and throws it behind the speakers.*)

LAURA: You ought to . . . put this on. The other's got dirty.

MAGGIE'S VOICE: Laura.

LAURA: Yeah.

MAGGIE'S VOICE: The boy, the student . . .

LAURA: Yes, I can imagine.

(*Pause.*)

MAGGIE'S VOICE: The journalist.

LAURA: Yes, yes, I know who you mean.

MAGGIE'S VOICE: He was in a bit of a state, I couldn't believe it. I think he must have juiced himself up.

LAURA: Yes.

(MAGGIE *sits up behind the amplifiers.*)

MAGGIE: He said your thighs are so beautiful, your thighs are so beautiful, well, Laura, you seen my thighs . . .

LAURA: Yes.

MAGGIE: I said please let's not . . . I'd rather you just . . .

(*Pause.*)

LAURA: You better go on.

MAGGIE: He said your body is like a book in which men may read strange things, a foreign country in which they may travel with delight. Your cheeks like damask, the soft white loveliness of your breasts, leading to the firm dark mountain peaks of your, Laura, now I am dreading which part of my body he will choose next on which to turn the great white beam of his fucking sincerity. Between your legs the silver comets spiral through the night, I lose myself, he says . . . he says . . . how beautiful you are Maggie and how beautiful life ought to be with you.

(*Pause. She cries.*)

LAURA: Don't.

MAGGIE: So. I don't want to know.

LAURA: No.

SARAFFIAN: Rock me baby till my back ain't got no bone.
(*He gets up.*)
After that the rest was downhill.
(*He walks away. She comes down.*)

The Second Set

ARTHUR, RANDOLPH, LAURA *and* SARAFFIAN *all wander out of sight during the first song. The band start an aggressive rock number; at the point* MAGGIE *should come in, they stop. Nothing. Then* MAGGIE *speaks.*

MAGGIE: Just try and forget, eh? Forget who you are. Don't think about it. Pack your personality under your arm an' have a good time. I really mean it.
Mama, take yer teeth out cos Daddy wanna suck yer gums.
(*Pause. Then the band begin again. At the moment of entry,* MAGGIE *wanders away from the microphone and picks up her bottle. Pause.*)
It's enough to make a haggis grow legs, man.
(*An abrupt drum solo from* NASH *and a couple of chords from* WILSON. *Then silence.*)
Now listen, kids, call you kids, so far you're schlebs and secret assholes. What you say, sir?
(*She listens.*)
Yeah, well, what you do with it is your business. Just don't ask me to hang it in my larder. Now this is meant to be a freak-out not a Jewish funeral. Let me make this plain. I don't play to dead yids. What you say, what are you saying, madam?
(*She leans forward, her hand in front of her eyes.*)
Sure. If that's what you want. Meet you in the library in half an hour. Bring your knickers in your handbag.
(*She leans forward again.*)
I am what? What is that word? I have not heard it before. What is stoned? (*She holds up the whisky bottle.*)
This is a depressant, I take it to get depressed.

Now I have some very interesting stuff to say. First we're
gonna talk about me. Then we're gonna talk about me. Then
we'll change the subject. Give you a chance to talk . . . about
what you think about me.

Right. So. It's mother born in Hitchin, father born in Hatfield.
So they met half way and lived all their life in . . .

WILSON: Get on with it.

(*Long pause. The band look bored and regretful at her
behaviour. She turns to* WILSON.)

MAGGIE: Wilson here . . . this is Wilson . . . on keyboard. Wilson
has always entertained the notion of taking his trousers
down. On account of the pain. So let's have them, Wilson.

(MAGGIE *lurches at the organ.* WILSON's *seat crashes over. She
climbs on top of him and tries to rip his jeans off.* INCH *pulls her
off, the others stand on one leg, play the odd note.*)

Right, let's have it, that's it, that's it, that's it, that's it, let's
have it, that's it, that's it, that's it, that's it.

INCH: Come on, come on now.

(WILSON *stands well away.* INCH *has his arms round* MAGGIE.
Then WILSON *slips nervously back to the organ.* INCH *slowly lets
go of* MAGGIE *then stands behind her like a puppet master.
Pause. Then superb coherence.*)

MAGGIE: Ladies an' genel'men . . .

(*Brief drum from* NASH.)

The acid dream is over lezzava good time.

(*The next number begins shatteringly loud. Where the words
should be* MAGGIE *sings tuneful but emphatic.*)

Yeah yeah yeah yeah yeah yeah yeah yeah yeah . . .

(*The truck pulls back upstage. The music fades and falters as it
goes.*)

YEAH YEAH YEAH

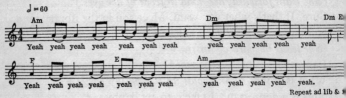

54

SCENE FOUR

SARAFFIAN *and* ARTHUR *straight in at pace. The music stops.*

ARTHUR: Great stuff.

SARAFFIAN: Really terrific.

ARTHUR: Where is she?

(LAURA *comes in.*)

SARAFFIAN: Getting her head kicked in.

LAURA: Didn't get us very far.

(WILSON *comes in.*)

WILSON: My jeans.

LAURA: Where did she get to?

WILSON: My beautiful jeans.

SARAFFIAN: Winner of the 1969 Judy Garland award for boring boring boring . . .

(INCH *comes in.*)

INCH: Wot the fuck was that about?

WILSON: Somethin' to do with the pain.

INCH: Wot pain?

LAURA: Go and get a shower ready.

INCH: Wot fuckin' pain?

SARAFFIAN: The pain, you know, the pain that makes her such a great artist.

(NASH *comes in carrying* MAGGIE *over his shoulder.*)

INCH: I'm not washin' 'er again.

LAURA: Put her down.

NASH (*swivelling* MAGGIE *round*): Anyone want 'er?

INCH (*stands on the table*): Will somebody tell me wot fuckin' pain?

WILSON: The pain.

(NASH *puts her down.* INCH *stands belligerently above them.*)

INCH: It's meant to be somethin' ta do with the pain. But wot pain? She can't even remember wot it was 'erself. Somethin' ta do with 'er upbringin'. Well, my upbringin' was three in a

bed and jam if yer lucky on Sundays, but I rub along.
Somethin' ta do with bein' unloved, but she don' wanta be
loved, she wants to be flattened by a Sherman tank.

ARTHUR: Leave it alone.

INCH: Of course, bloody Arthur thinks it's wonderful.

LAURA: Tell her now.

SARAFFIAN: What?

LAURA: Tell her, for God's sake, get it over with. It can't get
worse. She'll understand, she'll pretend not to, but get it
over with.

INCH: Wot a cow.

SARAFFIAN: Shut up.

(SARAFFIAN *goes over to* MAGGIE *who is propped up, lolling. You
don't know if she's faking.*)

Maggie?

(*Pause.*)

Maggie . . .

(*He slaps her face.*)

LAURA: She's listening.

SARAFFIAN: Some pressure building up, my dear, amongst us all.
The boy . . .

ARTHUR: I . . .

SARAFFIAN: Shut up. In his stumbling way. I, in mine. The band,
all in theirs. Arthur would like to be free of you. He would
like to set up a home with Laura. Yes. And you're sacked.

(*He puts his hand under her chin.*)

All right?

(SNEAD *appears with an Alsatian and a* POLICEMAN.)

SNEAD: This is a raid. You're all busted.

(*Blackout*)

INTERVAL

56

The equipment stands deserted on its rostrum at the back of the stage.
The speakers now have their backs to us.
    ARTHUR *speaks from the absolute dark.*

ARTHUR: What matter? Out of cavern comes a voice
            And all it knows is that one word: rejoice.

SCENE FIVE

The light comes up on ARTHUR *who is sitting at the front of the stage on a*
pile of champagne crates, staring at a small white box of potato salad in
his hands.
    The stage merges into darkness at the sides so that the characters come
and go in the night. First ANSON *approaches, jacket over arm.*

ANSON: I saw the second set. She rather . . . pushed the boat out,
    I thought.
ARTHUR: Yes.
ANSON: I saw the police about.
ARTHUR: We were busted.
ANSON: Gosh, I'm sorry.
ARTHUR: Mmm.
ANSON: That's terrible. Vicious.
ARTHUR: Vicious.
ANSON: Terrible.
    (*Pause.*)
ARTHUR: What's everyone doing?

ANSON: Who?

ARTHUR: Everyone.

ANSON: Oh, you mean the revellers.

ARTHUR: Yes.

ANSON: They've scattered. It rather loses its focus, you know. Till the champagne breakfast. It's . . . all over the place. The dinner tent's a disco and . . . they've got a Deanna Durbin in the buttery.

ARTHUR: Of course.

(*Pause.*)

ANSON: I did have a partner, you know.

ARTHUR: Yes.

ANSON: I rather lost track of her, I'm sure she's . . .

ARTHUR: Yes.

ANSON: You were at this college?

ARTHUR: I read music.

ANSON: What happened?

ARTHUR: I met Maggie. It seemed academic just to go on reading it.

ANSON: Yes.

ARTHUR: At the time troubador was the fashionable profession. It was also very good fun.

(*Pause.* ARTHUR *sets the salad aside.*)

Still the same shit-hole, eh?

ANSON: I don't like it very much.

ARTHUR: The people don't seem to have changed.

ANSON: Oh, I don't know. There are a few more totallys, you know. I should think. I share digs with a totally. I mean, I call him a totally, what happens is he has his friends to tea, I never stay, I just occasionally have to let them in the door and I overhear them, they're always sitting there saying, 'The whole system's totally corrupt an's gotta be totally replaced by a totally new system', so I just stand at the door and say, 'Couple more totallys for you, Tom.'

(*A Dietrich figure goes by in a long silver evening dress. It is* PEYOTE. *He is radiant.*)

ARTHUR: Hallo, Peyote.

PEYOTE: If ya 'appen to see a chick wiv jus' a pair o' jeans an' a leather waistcoat, say 'ello from Peyote, will ya?

ARTHUR: Sure thing.

(PEYOTE *passes*.)

ANSON: I'm hoping to drop out, you know. When I get my degree. I just want to groove.

ARTHUR: Course you do. But it's not so easy is it? I mean, the rules are so complicated, it's like three-dimensional chess.

ANSON: Yes.

ARTHUR: Just . . . work at it, eh?

(INCH *passes through heading for the tent*. ARTHUR *tries to get away*.)

INCH: 'Allo, Arfer.

ARTHUR: How they doing?

INCH: Still doin' the interviews.

ARTHUR: What have they found?

INCH: I don't know. I think Peyote swallowed a certain amount of the evidence. 'E's very quick.

ANSON: I wonder . . .

ARTHUR: Where you off to?

INCH: Look for some crumpet.

ARTHUR: Can I come with you?

INCH: You'd cramp me, Arfer. Somewhere in that tent is my ideal.

ARTHUR: What's that?

INCH: A short dirty-minded blonde.

(*He goes out*.)

ANSON: I've got a finger in my pocket.

ARTHUR: Ah.

ANSON: You know I'm a medical student?

ARTHUR: Yes.

ANSON: Can I show it to you? I think it's rather a good joke. Handshake, you know, and one drops off.

(*He shows* ARTHUR *the severed finger*. ARTHUR *takes it and looks at it seriously*.)

I cut it off a corpse in the lab. Here. It's quite a good joke.

ARTHUR: Yes. Yes.

(SARAFFIAN *comes in with a silver candlestick which he tucks away in the crates*. RANDOLPH *follows*.)

SARAFFIAN: Here we are, lads. Za za. Small advance. In lieu of. It's ten grand to a spent rubber we don't get paid.

ARTHUR: You must be mad, the police are everywhere.

(ARTHUR *hands over some silver spoons.* SMEGS *on from the other direction.*)

SARAFFIAN: Well?

ARTHUR: Here, you can guard your own loot now.

SARAFFIAN: What did they say to you?

SMEGS: Same as everyone. Name and address and not to leave the area.

SARAFFIAN: Do you know what they found?

SMEGS: Apparently that Alsatian went berserk. It found so much stuff its eyes kept crossing and its knees caved in.

SARAFFIAN: Where's Nash?

SMEGS: Gone for a smoke in the bog. Said he needed a joint to calm himself down.

(SMEGS *takes loot from his pocket.*)

SMEGS: Pepperpot.

SARAFFIAN: Ta.

ARTHUR: And Maggie?

(SARAFFIAN *looks at* SMEGS.)

SARAFFIAN: They can't find her. Disappeared. Don't say 'oh God', that's what she wants you to say. That's what you're programmed to say, Arthur.

(SARAFFIAN *holds up a hand to interrupt.*)

ARTHUR: Where is she?

SARAFFIAN: After the bust she just slipped off . . .

ARTHUR: Saraffian.

SARAFFIAN: Listen. She is sacked. Keep your nerve. Arthur.

(*Pause.* ARTHUR *glares at him.*)

RANDOLPH: Guv, can I . . .

SARAFFIAN: Here's something. Look. You have to get the little ball in the hole.

(SARAFFIAN *has taken a toy from his pocket.* RANDOLPH *sits down and tries to get the ball in the hole.* ARTHUR *watches, then turns to* ANSON.)

RANDOLPH: Right.

ARTHUR: Do you know how Saraffian made his money?

SMEGS: Not us.

ARTHUR: No, real money.

SARAFFIAN: Go on.

ARTHUR: He used to wait for some black group to do well in the States, you know like the Temptations, then he says he's bringing them over. Sell out, of course. Except when they arrive they aren't quite the same people they are in the States. They're just five guys he's met in a bar.

SARAFFIAN (*smiles*): This is true.

ARTHUR: Who he calls the Fabulous Temptations, then teaches them the songs the real group plays.

SARAFFIAN: I've brought over some great sounds this way.

ARTHUR: And in England nobody knows the difference.

SARAFFIAN: Seeing how they're black.
(*He laughs.*)

ARTHUR: Yeah, you wouldn't try it with the Beach Boys would you?

SARAFFIAN: Well, one or two cheap tricks it's true. People expect it. The odd artist hung upside down from a third-floor window. It's part of the show.

ARTHUR: No doubt.

SARAFFIAN: And Arthur feels strongly that . . .

ARTHUR: All right.

SARAFFIAN: No, come on, you feel strongly that . . .

ARTHUR: It's not worth saying. Nothing's worth saying. It's all so obvious.

SMEGS: Anyone got a fag?
(*Pause.*)

ANSON: Gertrude Stein never put her car in reverse.
(*Pause.*)

ARTHUR: Yes, there is the inkling of an objection, just a smudge, perhaps the feeling Al Capone might greet you in the street.

SARAFFIAN: I told you.

ARTHUR: Of course, it's a big organization, fair number of clients, so if some junior oddball wants to drive her band until they're catatonic with fatigue, with pills, with petrol fumes, well, at least that is her taken care of, until you choose to flick her off your balance sheet.
(WILSON *comes in.*)

ARTHUR: And if the damage is in the head and irreversible, well at least you were many miles away.

WILSON: Wot's 'appenin'?

SMEGS: Cambridge Union Debate.

WILSON: Oh. Wot's the subject?

ARTHUR: Ethics.

WILSON: County Championship?

SMEGS: No, no, not Ethex like Thuthex, ethics like—what you're meant to do.

ARTHUR: I'm going to go and find her. Take this.

(ARTHUR *hands* SARAFFIAN *the finger. Goes out.*)

ANSON: It's my finger.

SARAFFIAN: Course it is, lad.

ANSON: I get screwed up you know. If you can imagine my life.

SARAFFIAN: Mmm.

(*He smiles at him and wanders away.*)

ANSON: I just long to get away. Join a band. On the road. Eh? I wouldn't mind how menial . . . anything. It's just every day here I know what the next day will be like. Isn't that dreadful? Going to lectures. Work in the lab. And all the time I want my mind to float free, I want it above me like a kite, and instead it's . . . why have I no friends? And why does nobody talk to me?

(*Pause. He looks round.*)

And, of course, I'm being boring.

(*He turns and goes out.*)

WILSON: Bloody 'ellfire.

SARAFFIAN: Well.

WILSON: Never go to the piss'ouse wiv that one, 'e'd chop it off soon as look at yer.

SARAFFIAN: He's just lonely.

WILSON: Wot else 'as 'e got in 'is pocket, bits of old toe 'n' little chunks of earlobe?

SARAFFIAN: He's trying to be interesting, you know. Have some character. The man who goes round with a finger in his pocket. Very casual, very interesting. Rather dark. He just wants to be liked.

WILSON: You know the real killers?

SARAFFIAN: Yes.

WILSON: The ones who jus' wanna be liked.

(ARTHUR *reappears upstage.*)

ARTHUR: Where is she? She's not in the tent.

SARAFFIAN: Nobody knows.

WILSON: 'Where is she, wot is she on?'

ARTHUR: Where is she?

SARAFFIAN: Look in the common room. Or the cricket pavilion.
    She might be there. But don't let her know you're looking.

(ARTHUR *goes out.*)

    Nice boy.

SMEGS: Yeah.

WILSON: Let's 'avva look at that.

SMEGS: How long till we play?

(WILSON *wanders upstage with the finger.*)

SARAFFIAN: The first day they met he drove her to the north of
    Scotland. The northern sky was wide and open so that strange
    Hebridean light came through white blinds on to their bed in
    a perfect square. A perfect white square in a dark hotel room.
    And they felt that first night they were almost not in the
    world at all.

(*He smiles.*)

    I can give you more. Much more. Many more moments of . . .
    one thing or another. Arthur is obsessed. What happened in
    rooms. On trains. The telegram she sent. Some pair of shoes.
    Everything.

SMEGS: How do you know?

SARAFFIAN: Oh, she used to tell you.

SMEGS: Why?

SARAFFIAN: To make you think it didn't matter to her. That's why
    she told you. As a hedge against disaster. Like her whole life.

SMEGS: What gets me is, it's her we talk about all the time, but it's
    Peyote'll actually kill himself.

(LAURA *appears.*)

LAURA: Has anyone seen Arthur?

SARAFFIAN: Oh jeepers.

WILSON: Where is 'e? Wot is 'e on?

LAURA: I just wondered if anyone had seen him.

SMEGS: The footsteps go from left to right. Stop there briefly. Then we say . . .

SARAFFIAN: Try the common room.

SMEGS: Or the cricket pavilion.

SARAFFIAN: But don't let him know you're looking.

SMEGS: You look puzzled and depart.

LAURA: What?

SMEGS: Next.

WILSON: Laura. Jus' let me show you somethin'.

(WILSON *turns round. The finger is now sticking through his fly.*)
You see doctor . . .

LAURA: Wilson . . .

(*It drops from his fly to the ground.*)

WILSON: Whoops, there it goes again.

LAURA: Very funny.

(*She goes out.* WILSON *calls after her.*)

WILSON: Laura, I promise to concentrate next time.

SARAFFIAN: Where did you stash it?

SMEGS: What?

SARAFFIAN: The stuff.

WILSON: Oh, we only 'ad some giggle-weed, it 'ad nearly all gone.

SMEGS: Shouldn't we talk about the future of the band?

WILSON: Yeah.

SMEGS: Do something different, what do you think?

WILSON: I'd like to do some songs about Jesus Christ.

SMEGS: Wilson, he's been done to death.

WILSON: Ah—'is own complaint exactly.

SARAFFIAN: And who carried the rest, the hard stuff, who carried that?

(*Pause.*)

SARAFFIAN: Don't tell me.

WILSON: Well . . .

SARAFFIAN: Did she know?

WILSON: She 'ad a carpetbag. It's only Peyote. 'E used to . . .

SARAFFIAN: Did she know?

(*Pause.*)

She was the bagman and she didn't know.

WILSON: Yes.

SARAFFIAN: You think the police are going to believe that?

WILSON: It's true.

SARAFFIAN: Of course it's true, that's not the point. The point is, who gets to go to jail.

(PEYOTE *comes in.*)

PEYOTE: I jus' bin propositioned by the rowing eight.

WILSON: Wot did you tell them?

PEYOTE: I told 'em I wasn't that sort of girl.

SARAFFIAN: Listen, Peyote, you're going to have to come with me to the police, you're going to have to tell them about this bag . . .

PEYOTE: I said I'd smash a bottle in their face.

(PEYOTE *smashes the bottle he is holding against the crates. It shatters, leaving him with nothing but the smallest neck.*)

WILSON: Never works that. I never believe it when they do it in the films . . .

PEYOTE: Jus' who the hell do they think I am?

(*Pause. He is out of his mind and commands a sudden healthy respect.*)

SARAFFIAN: Yes, Peyote.

PEYOTE: I'm not anybody's.

(*Pause.*)

SARAFFIAN: No, Peyote.

PEYOTE: I'd rather busk, I'd rather play free gigs, I'd rather busk in the foyers of V.D. clinics than play to these cunts.

SARAFFIAN: Yes.

WILSON: It's pointless.

(PEYOTE *throws his wig violently to the ground.*)

PEYOTE: An' they've ruffled my fuckin' wig.

(*Pause.*)

WILSON: It's pointless. You'll never get through to him now.

SARAFFIAN: All right everyone. Find the girl.

(*Blackout. At once* SMEGS *plays acoustic guitar and sings amazingly fast in the complete dark.*)

Don't Let the Bastards Come Near You

I come from the rulers you come from the ruled
We were making the film of our lives
And the media dwarves were howling for masterpieces
People were dropping like flies
The crew were on librium I was on brandy
Struggling hard to get through
And the days and the nights were alive
With the hatred directed at you

(*Eight single spots come up on* SMEGS, WILSON, NASH, PEYOTE,
RANDOLPH, ARTHUR, LAURA, INCH *as they join in the chorus.*)

> *Don't let the bastards come near you*
> *They just want to prove you're sane*
> *To eat up your magic and change you*
> *So I'll help keep the bastards away*

(*The spots fade and we are back in complete black.*)

It was in your dark night of disaster
We watched as you smashed up your room
And Spanish and I we decided
We just couldn't stay in your tomb
In the morning I drove for the border
And Spanish he stayed till the end
But he has resources of humour
To which I cannot pretend

(*The spots come up again on the eight suspended faces.*)

> *Don't let the bastards come near you*
> *They just want to prove you're sane*
> *To eat up your magic and change you*
> *So I'll help keep the bastards away*

(*The spots fade.*)

Now I don't like singing with sailors
And I don't like drinking with fools
But I'll do anything that I have to
Because I know those are the rules
I know that the pain is like concrete
And the road is lonely it's true

And the load that we carry is studded with nails
So this is my message to you
(*The spots return.*)
> *Don't let the bastards come near you*
> *They just want to prove you're sane*
> *To eat up your magic and change you*
> *So I'll help keep the bastards away*

BASTARDS

♩ = 116
Very fast

I come from the ru – lers   You come from the ruled   We were mak-ing the film
of our lives And the me – di – a dwarves were howl – ing for master – pie-ces
Peo-ple were drop – ping like flies   The crew were on Li – bri – um
I was on bran – dy Strug – gling hard to get through   And the
days and the nights were a-live with the ha – tred Di – rec – ted at
you   Don't let the bas-tards come near you
They just want to prove you're sane   To
eat up your ma – gic and change you   So I'll
help keep the bas-tards a – way   A –
– way.   – way.   A –
– way.   A – way.

SCENE SIX

The deserted equipment. At the front of the stage MAGGIE *is sitting reading a book. Her lips are moving. A bottle stands by the chair.*
   Then SARAFFIAN *finds her.*

SARAFFIAN: Looking for you. Everyone. Everywhere.

MAGGIE: In the library.

SARAFFIAN: Didn't think of that. There are some things you
   should be told.
   (MAGGIE *holds up the tiny book.*)

MAGGIE: Thoughts of St Ignatius. Look. Pretty thin, eh?

SARAFFIAN: Yeah.

MAGGIE: Poor value. Just whatever came off the top of his head.
   (*She throws it to him.*)

SARAFFIAN: Maggie . . . there's a problem with the bust . . .

MAGGIE: And I got you a trinket.
   (*She tosses him a napkin ring.*)

SARAFFIAN: Thank you.

MAGGIE: You can melt it down.

SARAFFIAN: I will.

MAGGIE: And pour it down your throat.

SARAFFIAN: Maggie . . .

MAGGIE: You really got me Saraffian.

SARAFFIAN: I know.

MAGGIE: You did well.

SARAFFIAN: The timing . . .

MAGGIE: I was going to quit.

SARAFFIAN: I'm sure. But I sacked you first.
   (*Pause.*)
   Are you hurt?

MAGGIE: Not in my overself.

SARAFFIAN: What does your overself say?

MAGGIE: My overself says: everything's O.K.
   (*Pause.*)

68

SARAFFIAN: Maggie about the bust . . .

MAGGIE: Why are girls who fuck around said to be tragic whereas guys who sleep about are the leaders of the pack?

SARAFFIAN: Why do people drink?

MAGGIE: Can't stand it?

SARAFFIAN: Wrong. Need an excuse.

MAGGIE: Ah.

SARAFFIAN: They want to be addicted so's to have something to blame. It's not me speaking. It's the drink. The drugs. It's not me can't manage. They want to be invaded, so there's an excuse. So there's a bit intact.

MAGGIE: I've never been addicted.

SARAFFIAN: No?

MAGGIE: This goes through me like a gutter. Even on heroin I knew I could beat it. I did beat it. There's something in me that won't lie down.
(*Pause.*)
You know I've always pitied schizophrenics.

SARAFFIAN: Oh yes.

MAGGIE: Struggling along on two personalities. I have seventeen, I have twenty-one.

SARAFFIAN: Like everyone else.
(*She doesn't hear.*)

MAGGIE: Do you know the purpose of reincarnation?

SARAFFIAN: Not exactly.

MAGGIE: You get sent back because you failed last time.

SARAFFIAN: I see.

MAGGIE: I believe all we're doing here is trying to avoid coming back. I think you get sent back because you didn't get it right last time. Basically. You get sent back for having blown it the time before. Well, this time . . . I'm not coming back.
(*Pause.*)
I was a Viking, I was a Jew . . .

SARAFFIAN: Ah.

MAGGIE: I could get you through the Sinai desert, no map, no compass. I'd know. Just like that.

SARAFFIAN: Really?

MAGGIE: Why don't people take more care of their overselves?

69

They just rub them in the mud.

SARAFFIAN: Yes.

MAGGIE: Why is that?

SARAFFIAN: It's a failing people have.

MAGGIE: You don't believe a single word I say.

SARAFFIAN: No. Nor do you.

MAGGIE: Con safos.

(*Pause.*)

Go to San Francisco, sing in a bar.

SARAFFIAN: You never would.

MAGGIE: Well, what am I going to do tomorrow? Tonight?

SARAFFIAN: I thought you had the little fellow . . .

MAGGIE: Don't patronise me, Saraffian.

SARAFFIAN: . . . the finger freak. What happened to him?

MAGGIE: I don't know. I gave him some acid, told him to get high.

SARAFFIAN: How did you get it?

MAGGIE: What?

SARAFFIAN: The acid.

MAGGIE: Oh, some creep. Liked the way I sang.

SARAFFIAN: Have the police talked to you?

MAGGIE: I'm O.K. Don't worry. I'm cool. This is legal and it's all
I've got.

(*She shows him the bottle and smiles.*)

SARAFFIAN: Maggie.

MAGGIE: You're not my manager now.

SARAFFIAN: No.

(*They both smile.*)

MAGGIE: Do you know why I liked you as my manager?

SARAFFIAN: I have a fairly shrewd idea.

MAGGIE: Because you were such an unspeakable shit.

SARAFFIAN: That's right. I was aware of that. You'd say to people,
I'd love to do your charity gig, play free in the streets of
Glasow, great but—er—that bastard Saraffian would just
never let me. And everyone says, poor girl.

MAGGIE: You're right.

SARAFFIAN: I know. That's why everyone likes to be handled by
me. I'm an excuse. Any artist stands next to me looks like a
saint. Canonization. Cheap at twenty per cent.

MAGGIE: Then why did you like me?

SARAFFIAN: I don't know. Two-bit band, one of five hundred, fifteen hundred. Your tunes were better and the singer had balls. But where did I get you? One week in the *Melody Maker* at number eighty-four. And what's called a minor cult. I'd rather have leprosy than a minor cult. You know, some booking manager rings you, says what've you got? I say Maggie Frisby's lot, he says, no no, I never take minor cults. You have it round your neck in letters of stone.

MAGGIE: So what happened?

SARAFFIAN: Well. What happens to everyone? Bands just break up. Travel too much. Drop too much acid. Fifty-seven varieties of clap. Become too successful—never your problem, my dear—they break up because they don't feel any need. I don't mean fame, that's boring, or money, that's a cliché, of course it goes without saying that money will separate you from the things you want to sing about, we all know that. I mean—need. Maggie. Where's the need?

MAGGIE: I don't know. What do you think?

SARAFFIAN: I don't know. I don't sing.

(*Pause.*)

MAGGIE: It's nothing to do with singing.

SARAFFIAN: No?

MAGGIE: Oh, come on, it's nothing to do with being an artist, artists are just like everyone else . . .

SARAFFIAN: Then what . . .

MAGGIE: I have this sense of arbitrariness you know. Like it was Arthur but it could have been one of ten thousand others.

SARAFFIAN: Just . . .

MAGGIE: Where did we get this idea that one human being's more interesting than another?

(*Pause.*)

Saraffian. In Russia the peasants could not speak of the past without crying. What have we ever known?

(*Pause.*)

My aunt's garden led down to a river. It was the Thames, but so small and green and thick with reeds you wouldn't recognize it. It was little more than a spring. I was staying there,

71

I was six, I think, I had a village there by the riverbank,
doll village with village shop, selling jelly beans, little huts,
little roads. I took the local priest down there, I wanted him
to consecrate the little doll church. The sun was shining and
he took my head in his hands. He said, inside this skull the
most beautiful piece of machinery that god ever made. He
said, a fair-haired English child, you will think and feel the
finest things in the world. The sun blazed and his hands
enclosed my whole skull.
(*She smiles, pours whisky over her head, down her front, and
inside her trousers. Then goes over to* SARAFFIAN, *takes hold of
him. Puts her hands round his head. Then she lets go.*)
Saraffian. Thank you. Great relationship. Great creative
control.

SARAFFIAN: Maggie.

MAGGIE: Great help in career at time most needed. Never
forgotten. Farewell.

SARAFFIAN: Maggie. The band didn't get around to telling you.
They stashed all their stuff in your bag. That means the bust
sort of settles on you.
(*Long pause.* MAGGIE *turns back and looks at him.*)

MAGGIE: O.K. Try prison for a while, why not?
(*She sits down where she is. Pause. Then she lies down.*)

SARAFFIAN: Ah. Is that all right?
(*Pause. You can see him thinking. Then he takes some fags out
and goes over to her.*)

SARAFFIAN: Cigarette?

MAGGIE: No.

SARAFFIAN: You know . . .
(*Pause.*)
You know how people crap on about Hollywood in the
thirties.

MAGGIE: Yes.

SARAFFIAN: Long books about Thalberg and Louis B. Mayer. Who
laid the ice-cubes on Jean Harlow's nipples? But nobody
notices they're living through something just as rich, just as
lovely. And in thirty years' time they'll write books about
the record business of the fifties or sixties. What it was like

to have known Jerry Wexler. Or glimpse Chuck Berry at the other end of the room.

MAGGIE: You think?

SARAFFIAN: I'm banking on it. If I'm to have had any life at all. It's going to look so special. Once it's over, of course.

(*Pause. Then* INCH *comes on holding up one hand.*)

INCH: Upper-class cunt, it's in a world of its own. Smell my fingers.

SARAFFIAN: Thank you, no.

INCH: Dab some be'ind yer ears.

SARAFFIAN: Inch . . .

(INCH *sits down with a vacuum flask and a Mars bar.*)

INCH: Now I'm 'ungry.

SARAFFIAN: They should invent a machine.

INCH: Wot?

SARAFFIAN: Gratify all your senses at once.

INCH: Well, I did know someone used to eat Complan sittin' on the can. 'E was into 'is 'ead, you see, despised the body, so 'e reckoned it best to sit shovellin' it in at one end and pushin' it out at the other, an' that way get the 'ole job over with. Now I reckon if 'e coulda jus' spared 'is left 'and as well . . .

SARAFFIAN: Quite.

INCH: Do the lot in one go.

SARAFFIAN: Yes. The rest of us, well, we spread our pleasures so thin.

(LAURA *comes in.*)

LAURA: What's happening?

SARAFFIAN: Did you find him?

LAURA: No. Is she all right?

(MAGGIE *is lying still on the ground.*)

SARAFFIAN: Yes. Get ready for the third set.

LAURA: It's cancelled. There are notices all over saying it's cancelled by popular demand.

INCH: Great.

SARAFFIAN: I knew it. It's in the contract. Three sets or we don't get paid.

LAURA: So what do we do?

SARAFFIAN: Play it. Just play it, it's our only chance of the cash. I

73

don't care if nobody's listening. Why don't you round up the band?

LAURA: It's not my job.

INCH: I'm 'avin' me tea.

SARAFFIAN: Laura. Please.

(*She goes out to start looking.*)

Getting your hands on it. I mean, actually getting your hands on the cash. That is the only skill. Really. The only skill in music.

(*From offstage the sound of* PEYOTE *playing the piano with his feet. He is wheeled on by* WILSON, NASH *and* SMEGS *as* SARAFFIAN *goes out.*)

PEYOTE: 'Ere we are.

INCH: That's not ours.

PEYOTE: Saraffian said nick somethin', I nicked somethin'.

INCH: We can't nick that, we can't get it in the van.

PEYOTE: Let's 'ave a ball of our own.

WILSON: Did yer talk to the pigs?

PEYOTE: Let's 'ave a party.

(LAURA *returns.*)

LAURA: Right. Is everyone ready?

WILSON: 'Ow yer feelin', Peyote?

PEYOTE: Fantastic. Let's 'avva party.

LAURA: It's three-thirty, let's just play the . . .

WILSON: 'E's right back up there, 'ow does 'e do it?

PEYOTE: Listen, mate, if you'd dropped as much stuff as me . . .

SMEGS: It always comes back to this.

PEYOTE: You lot'll never understand . . .

SMEGS: If there's one thing I really despise it's psychedelic chauvinism . . .

PEYOTE: I want some fun.

SMEGS: 'I've had more trips than you.'

PEYOTE: Fun.

INCH: If you like I can . . .

WILSON: Wot?

INCH: Set light to my fart.

NASH: Oh no.

WILSON: Not again.

NASH: We've seen it.

WILSON: Dozens of times.

SMEGS: One streak of blue flame and it's over.

WILSON: Can't you do anything else?

INCH: Yeah. I do bird impressions.

SMEGS: Really?

INCH: Yeah. I eat worms.

(SARAFFIAN *returns with a conductor's baton which he taps on the piano*.)

SARAFFIAN: Right. Look lively, everyone. Third set. Any ideas? Requests?

WILSON: I would like to 'ear Richard Tauber sing 'Yew Are My 'eart's Desire.'

NASH: Wot is this?

SMEGS: Get in a line.

PEYOTE: Let's get on with it . . .

SARAFFIAN: This is the third set.

PEYOTE: I'm gonna need a fuck in about forty-five seconds.

NASH: Did you take sweeties again?

(RANDOLPH *has appeared*.)

RANDOLPH: Guv, this little ball it just won't go in . . .

SARAFFIAN: Keep trying.

NASH: Who's the vocals?

SARAFFIAN: Just stay in a line.

PEYOTE: I'm not gonna last.

WILSON: Listen, we gotta 'ave real vocals.

SARAFFIAN: Tony. Sing with the band.

RANDOLPH: But I gotta try and . . .

SARAFFIAN: You may stop. You may sing with the band.

RANDOLPH: Wot key are we in?

(*A photographic moment. Held for a second, the new team with* RANDOLPH *at the centre. Then the music begins with* SMEGS *on jew's harp, the rest come in one by one. An improvised jam, very inspired*.)

Let's Have a Party

PEYOTE: Ball gown baby
Bubble gum queen
Left her body
In my new blue jeans
Said hello
That was that
Didn't have time to check my hat
So

BAND: *Let's have a party, let's paint the town*
Let's have a party, chase away that frown
Let's have a party, let your hair down.

(*Instrumental verse, then.*)

Let's have a party, etc.

Ball gown baby
Bubble gum queen
Saw her picture in a magazine
Said she'd go down
The butterfly flicks
All of them changes all of them licks
So

Let's have a party, etc.

(*They leap back, challenging* RANDOLPH *to enter the song. He does, falteringly, inventing the words as he goes.*)

RANDOLPH: Ball gown baby
Bubble gum queen
Spread some sauce on my baked beans
Said hey I got you
Special treat
Be bop a lula
You eat meat
So

(*He is accepted. They all bash hell out of the piano.*)

ALL: *Let's have a party*, etc.

(SARAFFIAN *stops them.*)

Ball gown ba-by Bub-ble gum queen Left her bo-dy in my

new blue jeans Said hel-lo That was that

Did-n't have time to check my hat so Let's have a par-ty Let's

paint the town Let's have a par-ty Chase a-way that frown

Let's have a par-ty Let your hair down.

SARAFFIAN: All right. Hold it. There's no one to witness the third
  set took place. We need that little bloke. The one that booked
  us.

WILSON: The one wiv the finger.

SARAFFIAN: Yes.

WILSON: You won't find 'im. Some cretin gave 'im some acid.
  They took 'im to 'ospital. Stupid little shit.
  (*A pause.* MAGGIE *sits up. She looks at the band. A silence. Only*
  SARAFFIAN *doesn't see her.* MAGGIE *stands up and looks at them,*
  then goes out. Sudden deflation.)

SARAFFIAN: Oh dear.

LAURA: What happens next?

SARAFFIAN: Just let me think . . .

LAURA: What about . . .

SARAFFIAN: Tony, ring Mrs Saraffian, say I'm not going to get
  back tonight so she's to change the budgie's sandpaper,
  O.K.?

RANDOLPH: Will do.
  (*He goes.*)

PEYOTE: Are we gonna do this or are we not?

NASH: I'm beginnin' to feel jus' a bit of a fool.

WILSON: You think there'd be somebody. Wouldn't you? Don't

77

you think? Jus' somebody to hear us? Wouldn't you think?
(*They stop and look out into the night. Then* ARTHUR *comes in.*)

ARTHUR: What the hell is going on?

SARAFFIAN: Arthur . . .

ARTHUR: I just talked to the police.

SARAFFIAN: Don't worry, everything's in hand . . .

ARTHUR: They seem to think Maggie was pushing the stuff.

SARAFFIAN: That's right.

ARTHUR: Well, who the hell put the stuff in her bag?

PEYOTE: I think I'll jus' phase out, you know . . .

ARTHUR: He knows bloody well what's going on.

PEYOTE: Jus' go and get laid.

ARTHUR: He's a bit fucking selective about what he blocks out.
     (PEYOTE *shrugs and giggles.*)

PEYOTE: Well.

SARAFFIAN: Arthur . . .

ARTHUR: Did you tell Maggie?

SARAFFIAN: Yes.

ARTHUR: Does she know she's going to get done?

SARAFFIAN: Oh yes.

ARTHUR: Well, what does she say?
     (*Pause.*)

SARAFFIAN: Well . . . to be honest . . . she doesn't seem to mind.
     (RANDOLPH *returns quickly.*)

RANDOLPH: You better come quick. She's burning down the tent.
     (*Blackout. Pitch black. Silence.*)

SCENE SEVEN

Pitch dark. You can see nothing at all. You just hear their voices:
MAGGIE *is very cheerful.*

ARTHUR: Maggie. Maggie. Are you there?
     (*Pause.*)
     Are you there?

MAGGIE: Arthur.

78

ARTHUR: Ah.

MAGGIE: I'm here. I'm naked and I'm covered in coconut oil.

ARTHUR: Oh fuck, what was that?

MAGGIE: It's a rugby post.

(*She laughs.*)

ARTHUR: You've done pretty well.

MAGGIE: Thank you very much.

ARTHUR: Yip. Police. Ambulance. Fire brigade. You just got to score the air-sea rescue service and you got a full house.

MAGGIE: Thank you. What's the damage?

ARTHUR: Not bad.

MAGGIE (*complaining*): I can't see any *flames*.

ARTHUR: No, no, they're all coping rather well. They all love it you know. Dashing about in the smoke. They're hoping to make it an annual event.

MAGGIE: Really?

ARTHUR: Bit of fun.

(*Pause.*)

ARTHUR: How've you bin?

MAGGIE: All right.

ARTHUR: Haven't seen you for a long time. Must be six months. What have you been up to?

MAGGIE: Nothing really. I had the flu.

ARTHUR: What else?

MAGGIE: Do you have some cigarettes?

ARTHUR: Sure.

MAGGIE: Can you give me the pack? It's just if I'm gonna be arrested I'm gonna need some.

ARTHUR: Of course. Here.

MAGGIE: Thank you.

(*A match flares. We see their faces as they light their fags.*)

ARTHUR: What were you doing?

MAGGIE: What?

ARTHUR: The tent. Just making sure?

MAGGIE: Oh yes. Just making sure.

(*The match out. Darkness again.*)

ARTHUR: I can get you a lawyer.

MAGGIE: Don't be stupid. What else?

79

ARTHUR: Oh, you know. Larry says, come and see him soon.
Martha says will you cover the new Dusty Springfield for the
supermarket? Derek says . . . Derek says . . .

MAGGIE: Yeah, what does Derek say?

ARTHUR: Derek says . . . I don't know what Derek says. Far out.
Out of sight. Wow man. Jeez. That's what Derek says.

(*Pause.* ARTHUR *begins to cry.*)

I can't live without you. I can't get through the day.

MAGGIE: What else?

ARTHUR: You said you loved me.

MAGGIE: I did. I did love you. I loved you the way you used to be.

ARTHUR: But it's you that's made me the way I am now.

MAGGIE: I know. That's what's called irony.

(*Pause.*)

We better go back.

ARTHUR: Maggie.

(*She shouts into the night.*)

MAGGIE: Nothing's going to stop me. No one. Ever. Let me do
what I want.

(*Pause.* ARTHUR *lying on the ground.*)

MAGGIE: So much for small-talk. Will you walk me back?

ARTHUR: Right.

MAGGIE: Poor Arthur. You'd like to be hip. But your intelligence
will keep shining through.

(*She laughs, and they begin to go.*)

Watch where you drop that fag.

ARTHUR: Ha ha.

MAGGIE: Don't want to start a . . .

(*She peals with laughter. At once the lights come up. The stage
is empty. But thick with smoke. They've gone.*)

SCENE EIGHT

At once LAURA *wheels a flat porter's barrow on through the smoke.* INCH
appears from the other side.

80

INCH: I jus' drove the van across the cricket pitch.

LAURA: Well done.

INCH: I reckon it'll be takin' spin this year.

(*He and* LAURA *begin to dismantle the equipment.* MAGGIE *and* ARTHUR *appear.*)

INCH: There some people lookin' for you.

MAGGIE: Really? Where?

INCH: About seven 'undred and fifty of 'em. An' all round, I'd say.

(SARAFFIAN *appears squirting a soda syphon.*)

SARAFFIAN: My dear.

MAGGIE: Saraffian.

SARAFFIAN: Well done. Very educational. We have all learnt something tonight.

MAGGIE: What's that?

SARAFFIAN: Always put an arson clause in the contract. I'm going to have to pay for this.

(*He hands* INCH *the syphon.*)

Might as well nick it.

INCH: Right.

SARAFFIAN: My God, but that was fun.

(*He bursts out laughing and embraces* MAGGIE.)

Bless you my dear. At a stroke the custard is crème brulée. You've totally restored my faith in the young.

ARTHUR: Is anyone hurt?

SARAFFIAN: Can I tell you a story? I really must tell you a story now.

(WILSON *passes. He has scored a fireman's helmet.*)

WILSON: Congratulations.

MAGGIE: Thank you.

WILSON: It's really beautiful.

(*He kisses her.*)

MAGGIE: Better than taking your trousers down?

WILSON: Oh yeah. It's jus' a different thing.

MAGGIE: Right.

WILSON: If yer don't mind, I've 'eard there's a psychology tutor on fire, I'd really like to see it you know.

MAGGIE: Sure.

(WILSON *heads out.*)

WILSON: It's so stupid it's just wonderful.

INCH: Hey, 'old on, Wilson, I think I'll come and drag some naked women from the flames.

(INCH *leaps off the stage and follows* WILSON.)

SARAFFIAN: I'll tell you of my evening at the Café de Paris. March 9th, 1941.

(NASH *crosses with a bucket of water.*)

ARTHUR: You won't put it out with that.

NASH: This ain't for the fire. It's for Peyote.

(*He laughs and goes into the dark.*)

SARAFFIAN: I was with this girl. She's related to a Marquis on her mother's side and me a boy from Tottenham whose dad ran a spieler in his own back room. So I'm something of a toy, a bauble on her arm. And she said, please can we go to the Café de Paris, I think because she wants to shock her pals by being seen with me, but also because she does genuinely want to dance to the music of Snakehips Johnson and his Caribbean band.

(LAURA *picks up as much equipment as she can manage and goes out.* SARAFFIAN, MAGGIE *and* ARTHUR *left alone with the piano.*)

So I say fine, off to Piccadilly Circus, Coventry Street, under the Rialto cinema, the poshest . . . the jewelled heart of London where young officers danced before scattering across four continents to fight in Hitler's war. You won't believe this but you went downstairs into a perfect reproduction of the ballroom on the *Titanic*. I should have been warned. And there they are. A thousand young blades and a thousand young girls with Marcel waves in their hair.

So out of chronic social unease, I became obstreperous, asking loudly for brown ale, and which way to the pisshouse, showing off, which gave me a lot of pleasure, I remember they enjoyed me, thinking me amusing. And I was pretty pleased with myself. The glittering heart of the empire, the waiter leaning over me to pick up the champagne.

And then nothing. As if acid has been thrown in my face. The waiter is dead at my feet. And the champagne rises of its own accord in the bottle and overflows. Two fifty-kilo bombs have fallen through the cinema above and Snakehips

82

Johnson is dead and thirty-two others. I look at the waiter. He has just one sliver of glass in his back from a shattered mirror. That's all.

(MAGGIE *gets up and moves away to sit on the stage.*)

So we're all lying there. A man lights a match and I can see that my girl friend's clothes have been completely blown off by the blast. She is twenty-one and her champagne is now covered in a grey dust. A man is staring at his mother whose head is almost totally severed. Another man is trying to wash the wounded, he is pouring champagne over the raw stump of a girl's thigh to soothe her. Then somebody yells put the match out, we'll die if there's gas about, and indeed there was a smell, a yellow smell.

I looked up. I could see the sky. It's as if we are in a huge pit and above at the edges of the pit from milk bars all over Leicester Square people are gathering to look down the hole at the mess below. And we can't get out. There are no stairs. Just people gaping. And us bleeding.

Then suddenly I realized that somebody, somehow, God knows how, had got down and come among us. I just saw two men flitting through the shadows. I close my eyes. One comes near. I can smell his breath. He touches my hand. He then removes the ring from my finger. He goes.

He is looting the dead.

And my first thought is: I'm with you, pal.

I cannot help it, that was my first thought. Even here, even now, even in fire, even in blood, I am with you in your scarf and cap, slipping the jewels from the hands of the corpses. I'm with you.

So then a ladder came down and the work began. And we climbed out. There we are, an obscene parade, the rich in tatters, slipping back to our homes, the evening rather . . . spoilt . . . and how low, how low can men get stealing from the dead and dying?

And I just brush myself down and feel lightheaded, for the first time in my life totally sure of what I feel. I climb the ladder to the street, push my way through the crowd. My arm is grazed and bleeding. I hail a taxi. The man is a cockney. He stares hard at the exploded wealth. He stares at me in my dinner jacket. He says, 'I don't want blood all over my fucking taxi.' And he drives away.

There is a war going on. All the time. A war of attrition.

(*He smiles.*)

Good luck.

MAGGIE: Bollocks. I just wanted to go to jail.

(*Silence. Then* LAURA *appears.*)

LAURA: They really do seem to want you, Maggie. Can they have you now?

MAGGIE: What a load of shit. You're full of shit, Saraffian. What a crucial insight, what a great moment in the Café de Paris. And what did you do the next *thirty years*?

(*Pause.*)

Well, I'm sure it gives you comfort, your nice little class war. It ties things up very nicely, of course, from the outside you look like any other clapped-out businessman, but inside, oh, inside you got it all worked out.

(*Pause.*)

This man has believed the same thing for thirty years. And it does not show. Is that going to happen to us? Fucking hell, somebody's got to keep on the move.

(*Then she smiles, very buoyant.*)

Laura, come here, you look after Arthur.

LAURA: Yes.

MAGGIE: You can have your hat back, all the hats he wants to give you, you can have. Anything I said about you, I withdraw. The tightness of your arse I apologize. You're Mahatma Gandhi, you're the Pope. Arthur, you're Cole Porter. Or at least you will be. Or at least nobody else ever will be.

(*She smiles again.*)

LAURA: Shall I let you know how it goes in Stoke?

MAGGIE: If you make it.

LAURA: What?

MAGGIE: I'm only guessing. But I'd take a bet this band never plays again. When did you cancel Stoke?

SARAFFIAN: About a week ago.

MAGGIE: There.

84

SARAFFIAN: You know me too well.

(*He goes out.*)

MAGGIE: So I go to jail. Nobody is to think about me, nobody is to say, 'How is she these days?' Nobody to mention me. Nobody to say, 'How much does she drink?' Nobody is to remember. Nobody is to feel guilty. Nobody is to feel they might have done better. Remember. I'm nobody's excuse.

If you love me, keep on the move.

(*She heads out. She makes as if to take the bottle of scotch from on top of the piano but stops dead, her back to us, and raises her hands instead. A pause. Then she goes out. Silence.* ARTHUR *and* LAURA *alone.*)

LAURA: What are you on?

ARTHUR: On?

LAURA: Transport.

ARTHUR: Oh. Motor-sickle.

LAURA: Is there room on the back?

ARTHUR: Sure.

LAURA: Will you give us a tune? One of those awful old ones you like . . .

(*He stares at her. Then* INCH, WILSON, NASH *and* SMEGS *return laughing.*)

WILSON: That was the best night I 'ad in years.

NASH: Really brightened up the evenin'.

WILSON: Yeah.

NASH: I thought we was gonna 'ave a real flop on 'our 'ands.

INCH: Funny 'ow plastic burns in' it?

WILSON: Yeah, all sorta blue wiv little fringes.

INCH: And formica doesn't.

NASH: That's right. I noticed that.

INCH: I kept 'oldin' it in the flames but nothin'.

(*He starts loading the equipment on to the barrow.*)

SMEGS: So what do we do?

LAURA: The police said we can all bugger off.

INCH: Then we go 'ome, that's what we do.

WILSON: Great.

INCH: The van's over there.

WILSON: Anyone fancy a game?

SMEGS: Sure.

WILSON: Seven-card stud? I got some cards in the back. Perhaps we could try some new rules I got . . .

(NASH, WILSON, SMEGS, INCH *go off, pulling off the trolley loaded with equipment.*)

LAURA: Where did you put your helmet?

ARTHUR: I used to think it was so easy, you know. If I leave her, she'll kill herself. I thought she's only got one problem. She doesn't know how to be happy. But that's not her problem at all. Her problem is: she's frightened of being happy. And if ever it looked as if she might make it, if the clouds cleared and I, or some other man, fell perfectly into place, if everyone loved her and the music came good, that's when she'd kill herself. Not so easy, huh?

(*Pause.*)

LAURA: Play us a dreadful old tune.

ARTHUR: Laura. It just wouldn't work between us. Not now.

(INCH *returns.*)

INCH: There's 'ardly any petrol left in the van. I can't find the spare can.

ARTHUR: Maggie took it. To burn down the tent.

INCH: That's a bit fuckin' inconsiderate, she mighta noticed we was short o' gas. Lend us a couple a quid somebody. Arfer?

ARTHUR: Don't have it.

INCH: Well, sorry to say this, Laura, but we're gonna 'ave to sell your body. And pretty bloody fast. Somewhere between 'ere an' Baldock you're gonna 'ave to do it in the road.

(INCH *goes off.*)

LAURA: I've only waited six years. You might have mentioned it before.

ARTHUR: Yes. Yes. It was silly.

(*Pause.* SARAFFIAN *returns, picks up the situation at once.*)

SARAFFIAN: I had a look at the cellars.

ARTHUR: Ah.

SARAFFIAN: The stock is remarkable. The 1949 Romanée St Vivant is like gold-dust you know.

ARTHUR: Did you, er . . .

SARAFFIAN: Unfortunately, not. They'd padlocked the racks.

ARTHUR: Ah.

INCH (*off*): Laura, get your fat butt in 'ere.

> (SARAFFIAN *looks at* LAURA *who now has tears running down her face.*)

SARAFFIAN: Of course, this college was once famous for its port.

ARTHUR: I didn't know that.

SARAFFIAN: The finest cellar of vintage port in England. Then in 1940 when the dons heard Hitler was coming . . . Hitler was coming . . .

> (*They both look at her. She is now having hysterics, hitting the ground.*)

ARTHUR: Laura, can you stop crying . . .

SARAFFIAN: Hitler was coming . . .

ARTHUR: I can't hear what Saraffian is saying.

SARAFFIAN: They drank it. So he wouldn't get his fat German hands on it. Their contribution to the war effort. Four thousand bottles in just eleven months.

> (SARAFFIAN *as if to move.*)

ARTHUR: Leave her.

> (PEYOTE *enters.*)

PEYOTE: Fantastic.

ARTHUR: Yeah.

PEYOTE: Fuckin' on a fire engine, you wouldn't believe it.

> (*He goes.*)

ARTHUR: What's the time?

SARAFFIAN: Just gone four.

LAURA: When are you going to tell them?

SARAFFIAN: Who?

LAURA: The band.

SARAFFIAN: Oh, tomorrow. Enough for one day.

> (WILSON *has appeared upstage.*)

WILSON: Laura. You comin' wiv us?

LAURA: Yes. Yes. I'm coming with you.

> (*She stands a moment crying.* WILSON *looks at them all as if anew.*)

WILSON: I don't know why you lot make it so 'ard for yerselves.

> (LAURA *picks up* MAGGIE's *bag and goes out.*)

WILSON: Right. Well. Back into the little tin hell. Always makes me feel like bloody Alec Guinness. You know, into the 'ot metal 'ut. And at the other end, well we may be a little sweaty about the lip an' doin' that funny walk, but fuck me if we ain't whistlin' Colonel Bogey. Goodnight all.

(*He goes.*)

SARAFFIAN: Goodnight lads.

ARTHUR: Goodnight.

(SARAFFIAN *and* ARTHUR *alone.*)

ARTHUR: I knew a guy, played in a band. They were loud, they were very loud. What I mean by loud is: they made Pink Floyd sound like a Mozart quintet. I said to him, why the hell don't you wear muffs? In eighteen months you're going to be stone deaf. He said: that's why we play so loud. The louder we play, the sooner we won't be able to hear.

I can see us all. Rolling down the highway into middle age. Complacency. Prurience. Sadism. Despair.

(SARAFFIAN *gets out a hipflask.*)

SARAFFIAN: Don't worry. Have some brandy.

ARTHUR: What?

SARAFFIAN: Napoleon. Was waiting till those buggers had gone.

(*He offers it.* ARTHUR *refuses.* ARTHUR *sits down at the upright piano on the deserted stage.* RANDOLPH *comes in.*)

RANDOLPH: I rung the wife.

SARAFFIAN: Thank you.

RANDOLPH: Bloke answered.

SARAFFIAN: So.

(*Pause.*)

We must go.

ARTHUR: Who's the bloke?

SARAFFIAN: Where did I put the car?

ARTHUR: Who's the bloke?

SARAFFIAN: Oh, Mrs Saraffian's friend. Called Wetherby.

Secretary of the local golf club, I'm afraid. Mean with a nine iron. She likes his manners. I rev the Jag in the drive, rattle the milk bottles, you know, wait ten minutes, then . . . enter my home.

(*Pause.*)

God bless you and . . . Saraffian goes. Come on, Tony, long

way to go. Too late to count number plates, you'll just have to sit and think.

(SARAFFIAN *and* RANDOLPH *go out.* ARTHUR *alone on stage with the piano.*)

ARTHUR: Where is the money? And where are the girls?

(*Pause. Then he begins to play.*)

Arthur's Song

My relatives and friends all think I'm barmy
Because I went away and joined the Foreign Legion
My funny little ways
Have got the others in a mess
I think it's time that I came clean
Decided to explain
It isn't just the season
That has given me the opportunity to do
What I have always wanted to do
And though we're stranded in the rain
Leaving on a midnight boat
At ease upon our chairs before the mast
The world round is spinning round decidedly too much
We must hang on or lose our sense of drama

Never seen faces so empty
Never spent money so fast
You can't touch the important things
They keep them under glass
Your good friends always tell you lies
Doing what your bad friends would never do
And nothing rhymes with orange
But
I love you

ARTHUR'S SONG

Never seen faces so empty etc.

(Towards the end of the song SNEAD *enters carrying two suitcases. He comes down towards* ARTHUR *at the very end.)*

SNEAD: Sir.

(Pause.)

Left these.

(Pause.)

Left these behind.

(Pause.)

Sir.

ARTHUR: Thank you, Mr Snead. Why are you frightened? Why's everyone frightened?

(Pause. Then a blackout. Then projections large in the blackout, one by one.)

ANDREW SMITH NICKNAME PEYOTE

INHALED HIS OWN VOMIT

DIED IN A HOTEL ROOM IN SAN ANTONIO TEXAS

APRIL 17TH 1973

MAGGIE

ARTHUR

SARAFFIAN

THE BAND

ALIVE

WELL

LIVING IN ENGLAND

(Then)

Maggie's Song

Last orders on the Titanic
Set up the fol de rol
Tell the band to play that number
Better get it in your soul
Put the life boats out to sea
We've only got a few
Let the women and children drown
Man we've gotta save the crew

Because the ship is sinking
And time is running out
We got water coming in
Places we don't know about
The tide is rising
It's covering her name
The ship is sinking
But the music remains the same

Last orders on the Titanic
Put your life belts on
We can't hear the captain shouting
Cos the band goes on and on
I only want to tell you
That you have my sympathy
But there has to be a sacrifice
And it isn't going to be me

Because etc.

Last orders on the Titanic
Get up and paint your face
Deck hands in dungarees
And millionaires in lace
I only woke you baby
To say I love you so
But the water is up around
My knees goodbye I have to go

Because the ship is sinking etc.

The music remains the same

LAST ORDERS

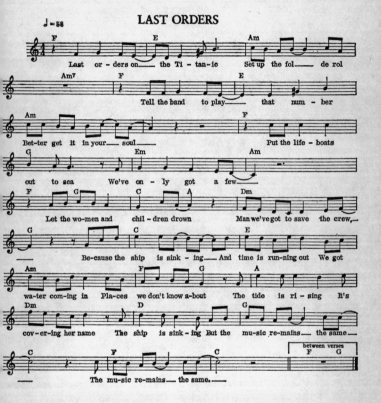

♩ = 58

F · E · Am
Last or - ders on___ the Ti - tan - ic   Set up the fol___ de rol

Am7 · F · E
Tell the band to play___ that num - ber

Am · F
Bet - ter get it in your___ soul___   Put the life - boats

G · Em · Am
out to sea   We've on - ly got a few___

F · G · C · A · Dm
Let the wo - men and chil - dren drown   Man we've got to save the crew

G · C · E
Be - cause the ship is sink - ing___ And time is run - ning out We got

Am · F · G · A
wa - ter com - ing in   Pla - ces we don't know a - bout   The tide is ri - sing It's

Dm · D · G
cov - er - ing her name   The ship is sink - ing But the mu - sic re - mains the same___

C · F · C | between verses F · G |
The mu - sic re - mains___ the same.___